NOT LOVE ALONE

NOT LOVE ALONE

A Modern Gay Anthology

compiled by

Martin Humphries

Stephen Bourne, Alan Brayne, Pete Charles,
Laurence Collinson, Steve Cranfield, Thom Gunn,
Lee Harwood, John Horder, Martin Humphries,
Mark Hyatt, Isaac Jackson, James Kirkup,
John Lehmann, James Liddy, Richard Livermore,
Edward Lucie-Smith, John McRae, Ziggy Marsh,
David May, Thomas Meyer, Carl Morse,
Philip Myall, Pat O'Brien, Felice Picano,
Neil Powell, Ivor C Treby, Nolan Walsh,
Anthony Weir, Jonathan Williams,
Anthony Worth, Ian Young.

This edition first published in November 1985 by
  GMP Publishers Ltd, PO Box 247, London N15 6RW

British Library Cataloguing in Publication Data

Not love alone: a modern gay anthology.
  1. English poetry—20th century
  I. Humphries, Martin
821'.914'080920664   PR1178.H/

ISBN 0–85449–000–0

Cover art by Ian Hands
Photosetting by Wilmaset, Birkenhead
Printed and bound by Billing & Sons Ltd, Worcester

Acknowledgements

For permission to use unpublished work I would like to thank the following: Stephen Bourne for 'Boats in Front Gardens', 'Shadow', 'Tricks' & 'Lost'; Alan Brayne for 'Look for the boy with the orange hair' & 'I launched myself on a joyride'; Pete Charles for 'Remembered as a Dream', 'Another Short Story', 'Lottery Ticket Seller (Alicante)' & 'Alluring (Waltz)'; Laurence Collinson for 'Irrelevancy', 'The Tricks of Transference'; Steve Cranfield for three poems from his sequence 'Music for the Soviet Minister of Culture (To the Memory of Dmitri Shostakovich)'; Isaac Jackson for 'on black performance art' & 'Homelife'; John Horder for 'In Memoriam Mark Howard'; James Kirkup for 'The Passionate Penisist' & 'The Swiss Post-Office Clerk or Winter in the Alps'; James Liddy for 'Epithalamion' & 'Menopause: The Lighthouse'; Richard Livermore for 'Foregoing Sundering Swords for Completeness' & 'For Cowards and Traitors'; Edward Lucie-Smith for 'Yes, I write this poem in', 'It's the season for broken hearts', 'Sleepily murmuring, not' & 'The Accusers'; John McRae for 'Poem?', 'When Did You Last Look for Your Father?' & 'Fall' from The Tunkhannock Murders, and 'Elijah and Isaac'; Ziggy Marsh for 'Fighting For Your Life', 'Lipstick Dreamer', 'Poor Old Athol' & 'Mr X'; David May for 'Observation 1' & 'Where Are You Now?'; Carl Morse for 'Fairy Straighttalk', 'Dream of the Artfairy' & 'West Street Story' from The Curse of the Future Fairy; Philip Myall for 'Eddie's Shorts' & 'Sirens'; Pat O'Brien for 'Winds' & 'Get Out'; Felice Picano for 'Progeny', 'Birth Marks' & 'Window Elegy 3' from Window Elegies; Neil Powell for 'Studies' (originally broadcast on Poetry Now, BBC Radio 3); Ivor C Treby for 'Image of Violence' & 'mosaic'; Nolan Walsh for 'After Five Years', 'monogamy' & 'Twisting Out'; Anthony Weir for 'To an Unknown Soldier', 'Damascene' & 'Minorities'; Anthony Worth for 'Hiss' & 'A Touch of Class'; Ian Young for 'Home on the Range', 'Adam and the Serpent' & 'The Alteration'.

For previously published work I would like to thank Thom Gunn for 'The Hug' and 'The Differences' which appeared in P N Review & for 'Bone' which appeared in the Times Literary Supplement.

For previously published poems the following acknowledgements are due: Grandma Press for Laurence Collinson, 'Reflections on Walking to Work Through Covent Garden' from Hovering Narcissus; Pig Press for Lee Harwood, '/Poster 2.', 'Just Friends' & 'Afterwords to a Poem by Jack Spicer' from All The Wrong Notes; The Menard Press for John Horder, 'Earthing', 'Hugging' & 'Professor Pott's

5

Strange Views' from *Meher Baba and the Nothingness*; Cressida Lindsay and Dylan Hyatt for Mark Hyatt, 'Nerves Blotted Out', 'There You Go Baby' & 'Individual' from *Equofinality 2*; *Blackheart* (Black Gay Men's Press) for Isaac Jackson, 'Michael Stewart is Dead' from *Blackheart 2: The Prison Issue*; Kyoto Editions for James Kirkup, 'Divina Commedia' from *Ecce Homo – My Pasolini*; Sceptre Press for James Kirkup, 'By an Unknown Photographer' from *A Sense of the Visit*; David Higham Associates for John Lehmann, 'Poem', 'This Excellent Machine', 'In the Museum' & 'The Rules of Comedy' from *New And Selected Poems*; The Jargon Society for Thomas Meyer, 'Letter From the Western Isles, Scarista', 'Valentine', 'By a Sleepy Lagoon' & 'Occasion' from *Sappho's Raft*, and for Jonathan Williams, 'Instances of Contemporary Meilikhopsthoi Amongst the Bleary Britons', '(12)', '(April 15) Seeds, Cotyledons, Clusters' & 'My Quaker-Atheist Friend', from *Elite/Elate Poems*; Carcanet Press for Neil Powell, 'At the Edge' from *At the Edge* and 'The Bridge' from *A Season of Calm Weather*.

Introduction

This is and it isn't an anthology of gay poetry. It is a collection of poetry by gay men. Men who range in age from eighteen to their late seventies and use a diverse range of styles, some who are familiar (known to many), some who are unfamiliar (known to a few), some who are published regularly and some who are published here for the first time. It is not a collection of poets from one school but of poets from different schools. The poems themselves reflect this diversity for they explore many facets of our lives. The common links are that all the writers are men, are gay and have found, or are in the process of finding, their voice.

But is it a collection of gay poetry? What is 'gay poetry'? Is poetry gay when written by a gay woman or man about their personal life, on gay subjects or themes, or when it addresses a gay audience?[1] It has been described thus: 'a gay poem . . . either deals with explicitly gay matters or describes an intense and loving relationship between two people of the same gender'.[2] If you accept this definition then this is not a collection of gay poetry.

Alternatively a poem by a gay poet which is 'about a painting or a landscape or (less tenuously) motorbikes is still a gay poem'.[3] I agree in that, for me, any poetry by lesbians or gay men can be seen as gay poetry. This is because i believe that our experience as lesbians or gay men is cognitively different from non-gay women and men. We live and participate however obliquely in a gay culture that only we know and recognise. 'Being gay is a universal quality, like cooking, like decorating the body, like singing . . . Gayness goes far beyond sexual/emotional activity.'[4] We have a culture that is our own. Often it is hidden and suppressed, our lives are a voyage of rediscovery of our roots. First we discover that we are not alone, that we have a history stretching far back to the dawn of time, and then we discover how language has defined and shaped us. Many of the words we use today were not words used to describe us centuries ago, but our language has roots. Our choice of words may not be accidental. In many ways we have to develop the skill to see what is hidden, to recognise ourselves for ourselves. As a whole this collection has a meaning which is not inherent in each individual poem. In this way it is and it isn't an anthology of gay poetry.

Not all the writers identify as gay poets. Some do, while others see themselves purely as poets. This reflects a conflict between politics and art. A conflict that will continue as long as being gay remains a stigma in our society. Some of the poetry is clearly 'political', for instance poems by Stephen Bourne, Carl Morse, Isaac Jackson. Poems by Lee Harwood, James Liddy, Thomas Meyer and Anthony Worth (for example) cannot be categorised in this way. The collection aims to cover many aspects of our lives, not just love alone.

This country, unlike North America, does not have a range of magazines, periodicals and small publishing houses which encourage the work of gay writers. This is why i wanted the book to include the work of relatively little known poets as well as those of established reputation. A desire to bring part of the underground to the surface.

In the course of working on this book i received far more material than i could possibly use. This has led to some rather idiosyncratic choices. Combined with my wish to find material that reflected more than our sexual/emotional lives i was seeking poetry that had a resonance. To this end i have in some cases rejected work which, though technically good, refused to lift itself off the page and delight or haunt the mind. It is clear to me from the material i received that there are many poets in this country committed to their craft; i hope that future volumes in this series will give them the opportunity to find their audience.

30 of the 96 poems have appeared elsewhere, either in magazines, periodicals or books. The remaining 66 poems are published here for the first time. Although most of the poems have been written since 1970 (some of John Lehmann's were written earlier) and many in the last few years, they do not necessarily reflect the effect of gay liberation. However, 'There are many dimensions to gayness, and especially since Stonewall, poets have been exploring the subtleties of these dimensions.'[5] Many of the poets here use wit to explore these dimensions, others use anger and some the role of a distanced observer providing a social commentary.

The experienced fragility of our lives comes out or is explored in the poems which touch on our experience of death. I can't help feeling that the current reality of AIDS has heightened the sense of mortality which surrounds us. Few gay men are unaware of death, often friends or acquaintances die early or unfulfilled because of the pressures of heterosexual society. Poems by Lee Harwood, John Horder, Isaac Jackson, James Kirkup, John McRae, Anthony Worth and myself explore these feelings.

Our vision of strength is often presented through poems of wit and humour. Poems by Laurence Collinson, John Horder, James Kirkup, Ziggy Marsh, Carl Morse and Jonathan Williams are good examples of this. Love also appears in its many guises. Some bitter, some brilliant, some unexpected. Laurence Collinson, Mark Hyatt and myself explore some of the difficulties. Those by Thom Gunn, David May and Felice Picano are observations of the realities of love. Those by Edward Lucie-Smith are lyrical.

Many of the poems are less easily categorised. Poetry, like many things, can slip and slide from meaning to meaning.

Editing the book has been a pleasure. I hope reading it is too. I would like to thank all the contributors for sending me their work; Philip Osment for listening to me; GMP for commissioning the book; Aubrey Walter for his support and encouragement; Crystal for allowing me to use their word processor; Gay Sweatshop for their encouragement; Ronald Grant for his comments on the introduction and for always being there when needed.

Martin Humphries
London, 1 May 1985

Notes:

1. This is a paraphrase of a statement made by Steve Abbott in his article 'The Politics of Gay Poetry' which appeared in *The Advocate*, 13 May 1982. The original reads: 'Is poetry "gay" when it is written by a gay man about his "personal life" (as Joe Brainard implies), on gay subjects or themes (Picano) or when it's addressed to a gay audience (Robert Martin)? Definitions abound and often determined a writer's embrace or rejection of the phrase.'

2. From the introduction to *The Penguin Book of Homosexual Verse*, 1983, edited and introduced by Stephen Coote.

3. Letter from Neil Powell, 28 March 1985.

4. *Another Mother Tongue: Gay Words, Gay Worlds* by Judy Grahn, Beacon Press, Boston, 1984.

5. From the introduction to *Angels of the Lyre, a gay poetry anthology* edited and introduced by Winston Leyland, Panjandrum Press/Gay Sunshine Press, San Francisco, 1975.

STEPHEN BOURNE

Boats in Front Gardens

You
Bourgeois bastards
Who live in healthy
Suburbia land
With your green bus stops,
Boats in front gardens,
Children who skip to school.
Emma. Simon. Jane.

Once upon a time
I loved *Blue Peter*.
An innocent child,
Deceived by the television.

Limited vocabulary.
Glottal stop.
'Chip' on my shoulder.
College taught me how to worry.
Caught between two classes,
Familiar with both,
Belonging to neither,
I was 'educated',
Then betrayed,
By a country which says
No.

A scruffy brown pigeon rests
On my fifteenth floor window ledge.
Far below
A vagrant rescues a dog-end
From the ground.

Today,
Amidst the bricks and traffic,
I am home.

Tricks

Underground
sit down
rush on and on
under the city streets
what fun!
I stare
at the passengers.
Strangers.
I try not to smile.
Once I was afraid
Of underground trains.
Not now.
I can go
wherever I choose.

I play
tricks
with my mind

pretending
to be
here,
there,
everywhere.
Him,
her.
In love,
in hate.
Fantasizing
this and that,
who,
what.
Imagining
whatever
comes
into
my
mind.
I have such fun
playing
tricks
with
my
mind.

Shadow

(written during the Brixton uprising in 1981)

Yes, I was a stranger,
a shadow on the street.
Now,
though my home is in the city,
it does not want me.

I came here alone
with dreams and fears.
My son,
born here,
now lies in a gutter
with blood on his fingertips,
tears in his eyes.
His screams cannot be heard,
or are they being ignored?
Another blow on his head
comes from the beast in blue.

I am alone
and the shadow on the wall
is a face,
pressed to the palm of a hand.
It is motionless.
I cannot help.
My dreams died.

Lost

His smiling face
Becomes distorted with anger.
He is an innocent victim,
Trapped by fear and ignorance.

Spread-eagled against
The cold, shiny surface of a car,
He is silently humiliated.
People stop and stare.
They do not care.
They will not interfere.

Nothing is found.
He is angry.
This has never happened to him before.

His home becomes a prison.
The streets are no longer safe.
His face,
Which used to smile,
Is lost.

ALAN
BRAYNE

I launched myself on a joyride

I launched myself on a joyride
in & out of amusement parks,
I strolled along the sweet side
of the street, where it was dark,
so I didn't have to ask
what lay under the mask.

I attended a fancy dress ball,
where we played a jolly game
called Cops & Robbers, & all
the good guy costumes looked the same,
so I didn't dare to ask
what lay under each mask.

I went in the Tunnel of Love
where we shared a beautiful boat,
but it couldn't lift me above
the shifting stream on which I float
for we didn't care to ask
what lay under our masks.

And so in the Hall of Mirrors,
where I wander for seventy years,
I smash each reflection to shivers,
but always a fresh one appears,
& I don't know how to ask
what lies under the mask.

look for the boy with the orange hair
used to be peroxide blond
but he's grown out of that phase
use to wear a gay lib badge
when it was all the rage
now he drives a Lamborghini
& his breath smells of violets
he smiles like a meat cleaver

greasy smiles will get you in the end my friend

look for the boy with the electric guitar
used to play for custom
round Graffiti Palace
now I hear he's halfway married
dazzled by the bright lights
stagestruck he poses profile
on the ladder of success

greasy smiles will get you in the end my friend

look for the boy with cannibal eyes
used to smile like sunshine
now his smile's turned black
he'll stab you now or fuck you
if you dare to turn your back
he's the cat with the cream
licking strawberry lips
his brain clicks up numbers

greasy smiles will get you in the end my friend

PETE
CHARLES

Another Short Story

NEW YK

So the first night I slept
in the apartment not
        quite above the apartment
where Gershwin wrote
        Rhapsody in Blue.
The lobby
        a marble hall
                seen better days
        it had.
Imagine
        Gershwin
                in that red elevator.
Maybe it wasn't red then
        been painted recently
                by the Super
so that
        blood from
                wino slashed wrists
wouldn't show.

Lottery Ticket Seller

(Alicante)

The old woman raised her blind
eyes to the sky
and howled a lament to the
god money

Up on the wall
I fell down from the cross
and held her in my arms

A legless man a distance
away waited for the sound
to cease

Remembered as a Dream

Tonight two sailors in a bar
came dimly through
One drunk, the other warm
No, I'm not like that, I said
So near and yet so far

I was only fourteen

Alluring (Waltz)

I found the piece of music
>   at the bottom of a dust covered
Suitcase in the depths of a
>   second hand shop in Camden Town
Bought it because of the cover
>   Edwardian lady with
Ostrich feather in her hair
>   *Alluring (Waltz)*
Martin brought it to life
>   on our (out of tune) Edwardian piano
Strange
>   a bit like Grateful Dead
Coming out of
>   that 30s bakelite wireless
With sunburst speaker
>   you found in Sadie's attic
And put a new valve in.

Reflections on Walking to Work
through Covent Garden

Obliterate this faithless street,
amputate my faithless feet:
every lilting stride I see
occasion for adultery.
Tree and vine assign their fruit,
soil supplies its gusty root,
that on this glinting avenue
fields may place their flesh on view.
Apples for taut teeth to chunk;
peaches in whose seas are sunk
voyaging lips; each moist grape
incites the tilted tongue to rape;
onions nudge me through their net;
golden sheaths of pith beget
golden echoes in the groin;
chaps and cheeks and cherries join;
potatoes' dusty rumps connote
a charming chubbier anecdote.

All fruits, all vegetables by
salacious innocence imply
canting pageants, truth that aches,
lies that heal, original fakes;
as: from the seed the growing sings,
from the growing ripeness rings,
ripeness rumbles to decay . . .
Let us gobble while we may.
Youth wears his secrets in each stare,
yet ask, and he is unaware
that through my metaphysic plight
he ploughs an earthy appetite.

He is a god who need not fly;
he stands adjusted to the sky
while I, impalpable, pace by:
a mortal hidden in a sigh.

Forgive me, dear, this daily lust.
Should I keep my senses trussed?
Does a reflex under cover
consolidate a captured lover?
These giddy pleasures are a game
fruitless in immediate aim,
but fruitful in the longer view –
my orchard arms reach out for you.
Infidelities of glance
are dogma of a greater dance
in which, embraced, our limbs are spun
past markets tumbling in the sun,
and aubergine and persimmon
and marble lads and we are one
until we graze against the frown
that creases this quiescent town.
The stalls and barrows are bereft:
only you and I are left,
except the ghosts, the irate ghosts
of the markets' darkling hosts,
observing, as the glitter pales,
the measure slows, the frenzy fails,
that we, with timid steps, express
our reassured tenderness.

STEVE
CRANFIELD

from: *Music for the Soviet Minister of Culture*

(To the Memory of Dmitri Shostakovich)

6

I am reproved once again
for retreating to funereal
gloom. But your objections,
like your cushioned rump,
    take full advantage of the shiny limousines.

Will you accord me the honour
of a lying-in-state?
I shall provide
a lesson in nose-holding
    for the lovers of integrity no doubt.

You will have the exultant
finales, as agreed,
but my music will continue
to shed tears,
    if only those of the long since broken.

7

My words have been harsh ones,
our enemies have found
no shelter amongst them.

Life is a spacious
apartment
with privacy and surveillance,

a journey West a not unthinkable reoccurence,
though my limbs are stiff
and hold no faith in such direction.

8

Some came to a terrible end,
some died in terrible suffering
and some in believing
in any case,
learning later . . .

Remembering my friends
and all I saw was corpses,
mountains of corpses.
I'm not exaggerating,
I mean mountains.

In happier circumstances
my mind might not have taken a morbid
turn. Not that I'd have lived for Georgian dances
either (God forbid!).
But 'the times' put the kibosh on that.

I force myself on,
tread the sly pavement
with suspicious feet,
the Russian *ulitsa*
is not an English street.

THOM
GUNN

The Hug

It was your birthday, we had drunk and dined
   Half of the night with our old friend
      Who'd showed us in the end
   To a bed I reached in one drunk stride.
      Already I lay snug,
And drowsy with the wine dozed on one side.

I dozed, I slept. My sleep broke on a hug,
      Suddenly, from behind,
In which the full lengths of our bodies pressed:
      Your instep to my heel,
   My shoulder-blades against your chest.
   It was not sex, but I could feel
   The whole strength of your body set,
      Or braced, to mine,
      And locking me to you
   As if we were still twenty-two
   When our grand passion had not yet
      Become familial.
   My quick sleep had deleted all
   Of intervening time and place.
      I only knew
The stay of your secure firm dry embrace.

The Differences

1

Reciting Adrienne Rich on Cole and Haight,
Your blond hair bouncing like a corner boy's,
You walked with sturdy almost swaggering gait,
The short man's, looking upward with such poise,
Such bold yet friendly curiosity
I was convinced that clear defiant blue
Would have abashed a storm-trooper. To me
Conscience and courage stood fleshed out in you.

2

So when you gnawed my armpits, I gnawed yours
And learned to associate you with that smell
As if your exuberance sprang from your pores.
I tried to lose my self in you as well.
To lose my self . . . I did the opposite,
I turned into the boy with iron teeth
Who planned to eat the whole world bit by bit,
My love not flesh but in the mind beneath.

3

Love takes its shape within that part of me
(A poet says) *where memories reside.*   [Cavalcanti]
And just as light marks out the boundary
Of some glass outline men can see inside,
So love is formed by a dark ray's invasion
From Mars, its dwelling in the mind to make.
Is a created thing, and has sensation,
A soul, and strength of will.
                              It is opaque.

4

Opaque, yet once I slept with you all night
Dreaming about you – though not quite embraced
Always in contact felt however slight.
We lay at ease, an arm loose round a waist,
Or side by side and touching at the hips,
As if we were two trees, bough grazing bough,
The twigs being the toes or fingertips.
I have not crossed your mind for three weeks now,

But think back on that night in January,
When casually distinct we shared the most
And lay upon a bed of clarity
In luminous half-sleep where the will was lost.
We woke at times and as the night got colder
Exchanged a word, or pulled the clothes again
To cover up the other's exposed shoulder,
Falling asleep to the small talk of the rain.

Bone

It was at first your great
Halo of aureate-
brown curls distracted me.
And it was a distraction
Not from the hard-filled lean
Body that I desired
But from the true direction
Your face took, what it could mean,
Though it was there to see.

When you, that second day,
Drew back the shower curtain,
Another man stood there,
His drowned hair lay
Chastened and flattened down,
And I saw then for certain
How Blackfoot Indian bone
Persisting in the cheek,
The forehead, nape and crown,
Had underlain the hair,
Which was mere ornament
– A European mock.

Could that be what it meant?
That high unsoftened rock
With no trees on.

LEE
HARWOOD

/Poster 2.

SLEEPERS AWAKE
from the 'sensible life' whose only passion is hatred

A red and black pagoda towers above the chestnut
    trees
in a Royal Botanic Garden
The lush greens of south London back-gardens
O summer nights when trembling with that ecstasy
our bodies sweat and flood one another's

Burst forth – sun streams forth – light –
all doors and windows magically thrown open
a hot lush meadow outside
with dark green woods at its edges

turn it another way
These are insistences not repetitions
or the repetitions are only the insistence on

and it all crowds in:

'Nostalgia for the life of others . . . Whereas ours,
    seen from the inside, seems broken up. We are
    still chasing after an illusion of unity.'
'Separation is the rule. The rest is chance . . .'*

which way to step?

and the dull brutality of monsters as they grind the
  bones
'forbidden to delight one's body, to return to the
  truth of things'*

*Albert Camus, *Notebooks*

Just Friends

Two men enter a Victorian House in Kensington and
  view a recreated Arab courtyard and a series of
  indifferent paintings.

Two men sit by Kensington Round Pond on a chilly
  autumn day and discuss the birds and animals to
  be found in cities.

Two men and a woman sit on the swaying top deck
  of a bus driving along the coast road from
  Newhaven to Brighton on a November afternoon.

Three men and two women stop to pick up large
  red-skinned potatoes that had fallen from a farm
  lorry, and then continue on their walk to see a
  tree full of herons and a lone kestrel perched on a
  footpath sign.

Two men walk on a summer evening through the leafy streets of west London and discuss renting a studio.

Two men stride along Hadrian's Wall in March and are met by earnest hikers in orange anoraks and woolly hats.

Two men walk by the sea at night.

Two men in the dark of a hide quietly lift the wooden flaps and observe the mud flats below them, the curlews, dunlins, grey plovers, cormorants, shell ducks, redshanks and herons.

Two men in Essex study an ancient church door with graceful iron work said to be Viking in origin.

Two men wave to one another (figuratively) at a great distance (real) and slowly fade from each other's sight.

Two men write letters to each other and meet, ride a motorbike, drive in a hired car, and take long train journeys north.

Two men scramble over a recent cliff fall searching for flints and fossils, and then fade in the sea-mist.

One man . . . the lush parks and mute statues.

At this moment I feel close to tears.

Afterwords to a Poem by Jack Spicer

(in memory of Bill Butler)

'They've (the leaders of our country) have become
    involved in a network of lies.
We (the poets) have also become in network of lies
    by opposing them.
The B.A.R. which Stan said he shot is no longer
    used for the course. Something lighter more easy
    to handle and more automatic.
What we kill them with or they kill us with (maybe a
    squirrel rifle) isn't important.
What is important is what we don't kill each other
    with
And a loving hand reaches a loving hand.
The rest of it is
Power, guns, and bullets.'*

      webs of lies upon webs of lies
a spreading mould of hate and viciousness
and death walking among us all

That mean spirits and the dishonoured man now
    hold sway
        poison us all with their intrigue and venom
Where no hand of kindness reaches out to touch
        our lips as we pass
As though love were driven out of the town
        and only left alight in the quiet of a home

*Jack Spicer, 'Ten Poems for *Downbeat*' (poem 9)

And you now gone 3 days with death
and now gone 3 days with death your big bear-hugs
your watch and chain, your self

We have no words to talk of you
to tell our loss
only the stuttered conversations on the phone
the broken phrases stood awkwardly round a kitchen
an empty cup in my hand

JOHN HORDER

Professor Pott's Strange Views

(for Margaret Drabble)

I was informed recently on '24 hours' (on BBC 1)
By one of our leading psychiatrists
Professor Potts, author of 'Hugging for Novices' –
He's also written for the T.E.S. on tribes in Melanesia
As well as for 'New Society' on the same subject –
That hugging should be made compulsory
Without delay, in all our schools and universities,
For boys and girls, throughout and after adolescence.

The Professor pointed out to me before the rehearsal,
Going up in the lift in the Television Centre,
That warmth and sexuality were two distinct
    commodities,
And that unless a teenager were actively encouraged
    to hug
Both sexes, he or she would be unable to sustain
    warm friendships,
Let alone achieve a lasting sexual relationship later
    on in life.
The Professor hugged Meher Baba, who appeared in
    the same programme,
And had been in India at the same time as him,

For over two minutes. 'Bloody perverts', muttered
    an envious cameraman.

Earthing

(for Meher Baba)

Earthing
Is a strange sort of thing
That can happen
Between two people.

Somewhere inside of you
You can caress
The other person's
Body and face.

Earthing, when it first happens to you
Is inevitably shattering.
Actually to feel that someone is there
In your presence

Instead of the everlasting nothingness.
Earthing
Is nothing short of miraculous
Is what gives you and other people

An inner as well as outer substance.
Earthing
Is what most people find most frightening.
Yet without earthing, you remain nothing.

Hugging

If I cannot hug you through what I write
I best write nothing.
It just can't/won't achieve anything.

But if I can take you into my arms
In what I write
(Or in the flesh

It matters not which)
And if you can hug me back
Through what I write

Or in the flesh
Then we may yet achieve something.

In Memoriam Mark Howard

You were English and middle-class
Charming and good looking
Without ruthlessness and guile
And you lived in Weybridge:

Your background was what killed you
Before you killed yourself
Aged twenty-six: to be English and middle-class
Charming and good looking in the eighties

Is to have only death to turn to.

MARTIN
HUMPHRIES

The sheer mindless brutality of it

The sheer mindless brutality of it.

Family enter with ease
decide who gets what, those closest
rail at police for permission to enter
when allowed are ignored, considered not there,
not part of his history.

This is our story echoing
through decades. Disregarded in death:
to us the telegram never comes, the deathbed
not ours to approach. Made of no consequence
returned to the shadows.

In death as in life, we
cannot quietly slip across the
river, knowing family will reclaim, unless
we change it, gather strength, take action and
make known our wills.

Piercing Heavy Velvet

Afterwards
playing with your hands
breaking sunbeams

Curled into your body
– legs across groin –
your fingers in mine;
playing with the light
as your lips drown my skin
disturbing the beams
as I think –
how little I know of you
how much I want to learn
– yet restraint
(for at our ages 'we must be careful')
restraint in case
we discover
a blemish
a crack
or dive too deep

So gently
I move your fingers
breaking the passage of light to my eye.

Recherche

(for the late Alan Harrison)

i caught a glimpse
just a passing –
centre to the corner
of my eye – glimpse
of eyes like yours,
in that instant i saw you
looking up at me
chunky knit jumper and loose smile

grief thick in my throat
eyes pricked with tears
for long moments i sat, face frozen,
rigid in the plain 2nd class seat
not seeing the countryside i was leaving.

memory awoken by a man with your eyes.

In Memory of Drew Griffiths

(murdered 16.6.1984)

You did not go gently
not willingly
it was a harsh and bloody 'birth'
Did it begin with love?
End in surrender to the dark
to the dying of the day
Or, like many another
was it bitter struggle lost?
In such birth is there continuance?
A refolding of the spirit
or is it nights cold stars
leaving only our memories
to breathe remembrance.
I care for your loss
the times now not to be
a future bereft of all
you were and might be
I rage at brutal fate
extinguishing your light
pity has no place
anger, sorrow, grief
mark for me, for such as me,
a comrade's destruction.

MARK
HYATT

Nerves Blotted Out

If you are my lover that pulses sperm
into my word crazy unbusiness-like head,
you will see how educated I am by tragedy
and how I spy at hate only to stand up,
but I will not be wounded by someone else's
endless triumph which dies mean.

You are my lover that fathers my womb
and polishes the ghost of my coward soul;
you only murder my face at the window
then hold my skin up to show street friends;
you stagger over me like an artist's rage
then clean out my belly, pounding kisses on me.

My lover, you let the wooziness of brutal love
zoom along my body squeezing stars out,
and I let you throw rotten apples in my eyes;
you make me go squirming through your bed,
but don't feel awful, because I do let you
laugh as you brush fur under my feet like weeds.

I see you as my ruin and within me the life.
As you spray the flesh with hot sparks
I hurt and howl then scream in hooked horror,
but I would never let my legs run from you:
I may go to hospital dressed in your answers,
but you are the gorilla I love to play with.

My lover, you are with the tides of mud
that splinter marrow with skilful pain,
but you and I are like that, without nerve.
In the masterpiece of your classic life
I remain the crushed pygmy of spirit season
the wild queer dressed up in freakish ideas.

If you are my lover and choke on whirlwind
blowing the dust of blues from your armour and
spit up the left-overs of experience like a servant,
well sometimes I am touched by mutual distrust
and the poverty of my head will tongue a snarling.
But my pawnshop love will stand each inch beside
    you

beyond the late hangings of life.

Individual

You are simply flexible
and the colours of your mind
look like feather in your eyes
you, always case solid facts.

You are the tapestry of much time
as you sleep like regular rocks,
in bed you are a wintery duck,
you just dwindle through my blood.

You are as pale as smoke by the open sea
and the silhouette of a beautiful soft breeze,
I find you lovely as sandy headlands
on the corners of natural humanity.

There You Go Baby

Agony under agony
it's making me
burn-up
I wish I could
hang-up somewhere;
I turn
minutes into hours
and life's a drag
without
this kind of thing
and everything
is so unhappy
really
I can't fall in love
because
it's a natural killer.

I dream & dream
of Harlequin
and I am having one
of those sexless nights
where birds fly out
of my mouth
with their tails
on fire.

ISAAC
JACKSON

Michael Stewart is Dead

(Michael Stewart was brutally murdered by New York City transit policemen in the fall of 1983. His eyes were removed and destroyed illegally by the coroner's office to prevent justice from being brought to bear on the guilty transit policemen. Michael Stewart worked as a busboy in the Pyramid Club, a gay-owned and operated club on Manhattan's Lower East Side.)

on the number one/going downtown to the garage/
two white cops/standin' in front of me/
description of crimes and suspects/blare out/
of his box/offending my sense/if it was my radio/
i'd get a ticket.

one sez to the other: wouldn't it be funny if/
when a call went out/the guy was sitting right in
front of you/wouldn't it be funny/and easy to do/
two against one/two hands against a gun/
it could have been me.

i waz living on the lower east side/a few blocks
from the pyramid/when i first noticed him/
picking up the empty beer glasses/pushing thru
the mixed crowd/gays/lesbians/straights/
bridge & tunnel crowd/shoulder to shoulder w/
east village artists/thin dreads hanging into his eyes/
i often commented to friends i might
consider trimming my dreads like his/
long in front/short on the sides/like the black guy

in/The Thompson Twins/'Hush my baby . . .
don't you cry . . . we have one weapon in our
defense/silence'/

at the fourteen street stop/on the 11 line/
doing my art in the subways/drawing sketches/
influenced by graffiti art/left no marks on the walls/
anywhere/working hard/sketching the
Statue of Liberty/leading the people/to some
billboard Liberia/i'm doing this sketch for the
anti-gentrification show/and this transit worker
gets irate/and rips my painting/to shreads/
Miz Liberty to shreads/screams/yells/tears/
i walk away/and live to complain.

i never knew his name before/i learned it by
reading in the paper/of the death of a young man/
a young dread-locked graffiti artist/in the
custody of transit police/following an arrest.

Michael Stewart is dead/and wouldn't it be
funny/if the suspect/waz already standing in
front of you/and easy to do two against one/
two hands against a gun/it could have been me/
this time i got away.

on black performance art

originally i thought
this wud be a show
up on broadway or gettin down
at the brooklyn academy of music

multi-media
w/ 20 ft. high slides
    (rear projected of course
        so as not to reveal nervous shadows)

i wanted to bring my synthesizer
and read poems set to thunderclaps
    and snow falling simultaneously
while an acrobat did summersaults
over the orchestra pit/ puttin knots in yr stomach

i wanted you to come stoned
to watch the highest technology
dance for a black man
but the slides all come back
to the bare brilliance of the lightbulb
i use to write with

and the only sound i could
'faithfully reproduce' was
the sound of my heart pushing blood
through the hollow fullness of my hand
shake slapping a calabash/ the sound of snow
    melting fast in the African sun

Homelife

the homelife of black homosexuals
is powerful when scribed for paper
or painted on paper
or wrapped up in gift paper
sent to lovers a month
ahead of time/ bookrate

slow down pony
for our generation
disco challenges the length of words
drugs/ the reality of feeling
c'mon slow down pony
dance dance slow down

four-eye generation
i & i strain
fatigue clothes and attitude
fungus & fungi
i'm straining to be strong
you got my body all wrong
strength is in the structure/ not
the size/ Surprised?
i didn't think so/ c'mon
slow down pony/ i want to fuck you

yes/ you are young
        but i'm not that old
my house is new and eager
for your impatience/ your further growth
sit
and watch my hair grow for you/ the sea/
hair and assholes all part

for us as we walk by/fragrant/ oily salt musk
that new york city smell
of broken animal eggs/ patchcords/ networks
          not the phones of LA
          or the streets of san francisco
          or the pretty boys of amsterdam
just us at home.

happiness is in the home
happiness is in the heart
i bring the disco into my home
i bring the disco into my heart
i listen to the radio
my voice is on the radio
my tongue is in your ear/
     then your asshole
i am ready/   i am strong
it is dark in your room/ darker than your skin
you're listening/ hoping/ waiting
touching yourself/ lapping up the air
from the antennae/ over the garage

c'mon on/ wake up
after i get out of work/ let's
catch a bus/ and ride up to the country
and fuck under the stars
my face above yours
blocking out the constellations
like an interstellar dust cloud
bright eyed/ like Orion's dog/ on
a Nubian night ride of flapping/
dusty dicks/ over into the morning
rising hot & heavy/ evaporated male nipple-milk
on our breasts/salt shallow seasonings of
love/ c'mon pony/ let's

run/ you half animal ifa spirit you/
alternating between lifeforms/ you
make bird music/ as i wrap my legs/democratically
around your back/ let me ride/ let me rest
i declare/ i swear
you wear me out.

JAMES
KIRKUP

By An Unknown Photographer:

'A Jew Hounded in Amsterdam – 1943'

I recognize those tall, respectable burghers' houses,
the neat, elegant façades, the worn brick pavements
of the canals, the wintry plane trees.

But under those tall windows and stepped gables
military trucks are parked, with helmeted guards.
And in the unnatural calm of the almost deserted
    street
six or seven young Nazis, booted and breeched,
smilingly observe an officer in long uniform
    greatcoat,
belted and buttoned, insignia blazing on peaked
    cap,
leisurely pursuing an easy prey – catching up with
the elderly, white-faced Jew stumbling towards us
in a cumbersome, dark overcoat or pelerine
flapping open on a formal suit, white shirt, bow tie.

They all have caps or helmets, but he is hatless –
black homburg snatched from his defenceless head
by mocking hands, or by the northsea wind
that stabs his thick hair as he tries to run away,
right hand outstretched in terror, as in a nightmare,
face blank with fright. He is hoping to escape, but
the long skirts of his mantle impede him, clinging to

his ankles like the heavy mud of a bad dream
in which his neat shoes seem to be treading
    quicksands.

I recognize him, too, and his laughing tormentors
who are about to grab this hapless victim and
    ship him off to the camps, the gas ovens, the
    crematoria
of Auschwitz, Dachau, Maidanek, Bergen-Belsen.
Their self-confident smiles are brutal in
their smug ferocity, as if they never doubted
their mastery, their right to humiliate, their
healthy aversion to all that is not Aryan superiority.

I recognize that Jew, my brother, for in him
I can see myself, someone apart from other men,
beyond the pale, hounded and persecuted too
by laughing tormentors – some 'gay', some of them
    Jews –
who never doubted the rightness of their cause,
or the universal humour of their mockery.

– That Jew is dead now, and I live on.
But the days of his tormentors are numbered, and
    soon
they, too, will be hounded to accusation, trial,
    death.
Some will escape, but be brought to justice from
every country in the world. Yet the lists are long
still, of those mockers and murderers,
those criminals against humanity who must one day
be given a taste of their own punishments.

We, too, have our lists.
And one day our turn will come.

Divina Commedia

The other day, Pier Paolo Pasolini,
one rainy February evening in Rome,
I retraced your final steps, your fall,
trying to make your martyrdom forever mine
upon the sad back roads of Ostia
whose grubby wildernesses,
the streets and sands of Teorema,
the rocks and ashes of your perfect Passion,
drag on southwards into dusty dunes,
the railway tracks, the runways of Fiumicino –
aeroporto landscape of Fellini, Antonioni and Godard:
but above all, my Virgil, my deliverer, the common
    ground
of terrorism, torture, treachery,
of idle crucifixion, and lust in action.

Barbed-wire limbo of the destitute, the houseless,
a Caravaggio country of desire's final anarchy.
– Alone I roamed from one grimy station to the next
of our long Via Dolorosa, scarred and scattered
with scumbags, broken bottles, bones and dogshit.
There on my knees I prayed for some salvation,
wishing in that Gethsemane it had been only me
you met that fatal evening in November –
not your Judas, but just your James, albeit James
the Lesser you picked up so casually about eight p.m.
even as, so casually, about eight p.m., you picked up
me, some twenty years before, my comrade, at our
    common
rendezvous with fate – our last, pathetic calvary
of fools, piss-awful, the shitehouse at Roma Termini.

March 1979.

The Passionate Penisist

In all the art museums of the world,
the traveller's eye appreciates perspectives,
volume, brushwork, colour, composition,
the peculiar elevation of a church, a house, a stable,
the bright blue background of yet another miracle.

The eye of the penisist, too, goes grazing
on acres of landscapes, but scanning
the village square, the docks, the hilltop seminary
for something more than just technique:
for the human touch he craves – for man.

Among the candid Flemish primitives –
the peasant hop, the farmer's wedding feast,
the skating scene, the tavern junket –
the penisist's long, pensive gaze
absorbs the crowded details, feels the pulse

of an innocence long dead, still mischievous:
but fixes not upon the broad face of the bride
tipsy beneath her tilted, hanging crown, nor on
the plump, willing servant, the girl pouring wine,
the pregnant wife – however charming, comical,
    agreeable.

Instead, the penisist must feast his eyes upon
the gallant grenadier, the good-natured gentleman
in bustling thigh-boots and feathered hat,
the fresh-faced youths at cards, that fellow
looking back across his shoulder, absently,

as he pisses unconcerned against a neighbour's wall.
– The girls are painted so alluringly,
and yet the artist (so the penisist perceives)
is just as interested in the boys and men:
their rags, armour, jerkins, leather gauntlets,

their fine lace collars and their crisp white ruffs,
their silken breeches, slashed velvet pantaloons,
their buckled buskins and their cambric cuffs.
These musketeers are more than ordinary men:
they are the passionate penisist's wet dreams.

With spread thighs unthinkingly, enticingly apart,
they loll, laughing, in the parlour of an inn –
an interval in war, or in the longer battle
of the sexes – flinging a ready arm around
a dimpling servant's gathered waist,

in the other hand a tilted cup of wine, a smile
lifting the blond moustachios on perfect, pearly teeth.
– But beyond the pleasant surface of the picture
the penisist perceives another scene: those two
drunken comrades, their arms around each other's
    necks,

the schoolboy friends, their hands beneath their
    desks,
the rosy satyr staggering up the stairs to bed
assisted by a strapping youth, half-naked, with
vine-leaves in his hair, and winking at the rest,
the battle-stained soldiers embracing in the hay.

And in the anonymous medieval scenes
of tortured saints and cruel crucifixions,
the serious penisist's concern is not so much
for the suffering Sebastian, a callow youth
with arrows all artistically placed, arranged

neatly to avoid the genitals, discreetly veiled,
nor for the emaciated, pallid, pitiful Christ,
as for the evil men, the villains, torturers
with ugly Spanish or Italian peasant grins,
mean-mouthed, dark-jowled, cross-eyed

and bearing all the instruments of death and torment –
the red-hot pokers, steel-knotted whips, huge pin-
    cers:
those muscular backsides that bend with bulging
    brawn
to pick up stones and sticks, to bend their bows,
those coal-heavers' handsome arms and shoulders,

and with those sumptuous thighs in multicoloured
    tights
exhibiting their gross, loaded, vicious, throbbing
codpieces, agape on savage engines
more potent than any whip or cudgel. These
are the visions of the penisist's dark night.

And these are the penisist's delight –
who feels released, uplifted, yet
saddened by the sight of all he longs for,
and may, or may not have the power to resist:
these are the passions of the penisist.

The Swiss Post-Office Clerk or
Winter in the Alps

(a cabaret song)

He's gay as all get-out,
and coping rather well.
It's no joke wetting stamps
when you feel you are in hell.

So why does he give me such
a bad time, play hard to please
when I ask him for a stamp?
Why does he suddenly freeze?

He doesn't come on gay,
though he works at it too much.
But when he sees me smile, and I say
'Airmail, with *pretty* stamps, to such and such . . .'

Why does he have to put me down
so distantly, as if I really were
from outer space, or sick with AIDS,
his frown expressing: 'God, get *her*!'?

Well, yes, I know it's self-defence,
automatic, self-protective.
That is his life, and this is mine.
But I'm no vice detective.

He has to live here. I'm
just a tourist passing through.
It's natural that he should feel
threatened with exposure, too,

should I do what I would like
to do, and breach all protocols,
and take him in my arms, and sigh:
'These heavenly Swiss rolls!'

– But between us stands the counter
like virginity's sharp sword,
so he wets and franks my stamps
without a smile, without a word.

And I leave the place depressed,
but hoping I've not been too bold –
for his was the radiance of youth, while I
am the gay who came in from the cold.

In the Museum

These little vases, made of earth,
Were, so the label tells me, used
To catch the mourner's tears, and buried
With the beloved at death.

The Greeks, it seems, believed that so
They sealed a promise to the closed
Eyes in the tomb that one day they
Would meet and kiss again.

Absurd: and yet I like this fancy
So characteristic of the race
Who dreamed a myth round everything
Mysterious to reason;

For tears, most evanescent of all
Tokens of love, are yet the purest,
And through their veil we glimpse the true
Arch of the spirit's action,

All accident that seemed to cling
Defacing that inmost design
In the constriction of extreme grief
Like rubbish burnt away.

I am haunted by these fragile vessels
Made rather out of love than earth,
Pledges of that warm human room
Where ghosts may find their welcome.

The Rules of Comedy

For Mr Norris, I must now admit
I have scant sympathy: a pimp, and crook,
The falsest friend, who landed in the shit
Simples, who tried to take him off the hook;

I am not Christian enough to share
The puppet Bradshaw's weakness for his sins,
And if there is a hero, Ludwig Bayer,
The selfless, never hoodwinked marxist, wins;

And yet how skilfully the author uses
This foible to complete the tale of fate,
And, in the rules of comedy, confuses
Neither the moral logic, nor ultimate

Damnation of one inviting Their pursuit,
The Kindly Ones, with their unfailing scent
Like wasps, for over-ripe and rotten fruit,
And, scorning pretty jokes and manners, sent

Schmidt to torment him: he deserved the beast,
But really one must feel some slight dismay
In watching how sadistic passions feast
On one who welcomed Annie's whips in play.

Goodbye, then, Mr Norris; changing trains
For one whose destination ends desire
And needs no luggage of ill-gotten gains,
You do not change the loathing you inspire;

And yet; because a masterpiece transcends
The shudders that its characters provoke
Re-moulding all to its sublimer ends –
I'm sorry you died friendless, ugly, broke.

JAMES
LIDDY

Epithalamion

I know nothing but this scene:
a farmer's field of grass
stalky and thistledowned
buttercups
cowslips
belladona-standing hedges –
an edge of sadness
. . . ghosts a
thousand years of horses . . .
and a trampled section a swarth
of a path on one side,
the one with running water,
no trees except on the far bank
(to swim in it naked for even a few minutes).
A slightly tilting field
on the road to Limerick
called Barrington's Bridge (I am sure)
with access to the wandering slithering
thickening slendering Maigue
to which the bards of Desmond brought,
tramping through the ragworth,
their narcissistic fears like piss
standing on the bank on their big feet
singly or monkey-chatting
until in the cool of evening –
if they came then – without caves
teeth-chattering started.

Anxiety the stalks running
through my body about the past
that is swept away like the Maigue
swept on by spring flood,
no punctuation no looking back.
(To swim in it, a fish in water.)
One sentence on it runs into another,
another bardic figure round the bend
or – what we want – a sensuous body
round the corner beckoning.
The dream bard out of the hedge
stands on the edge
and dissolves into poetry . . .
splashes a young nubile figure
in the parting stream.
My tired eye focuses there
the sensuous flesh becoming
non-bachelor wonder-past –
the river murmurs through its green
sludge . . .
A near naked army may
Have stood on either side
Pre-demon fighting with demon . . .
nothing carries your eye
back further than the blink of a river.
I place my arms around nakedness
Meaning comes on like evening.

It was an outing: frisky lambkins
recovered from breakfast
and cigarette-walk on the terrace
rampageous pigeons uncaged
blurring along the field path, for
a sports meeting then a picnic.
The under-14 hundred yards
a handicap event and I was a few

yards in front . . . togged out.
A start gun held by Fr Peter
for the hopping-flopping bunch . . .
I looked at the river at the trees
I saw the demons hovering
over the water – bridegrooms . . .
I decided to run (pounding temple
prickly arse) and poured over
the line first, a cheered hero.
One to whom men would speak –
a swan sailed by the river
singing like a bard on his death bed
like a bard who has been to the river
for the last time. O swept away too
the warm summer of Pius XII
as hot as the Campagna . . .
though a camoufleur I had run
like one of those over the flat grass
in the fields aside Anacotty
for the gold medal and I seemed
not like one who loses but
like one who's spun.

I learnt to sing (thank you)
and I sing before the painted
marriage chamber door.
By song not restoring the past
(puberty, the river, the garland
that is a lost medal) – desperation,
it's not even a task.
The initiation is to transfer sexual
purpose – everything that is energy –
into the creative not the sublime.
To be-hop more of a lover as you
incarnate better the poet.
To be more flowing more of a river sensualist.

Menopause: The Lighthouse

Concupiscences, my sister, zinged me. Ah me!

No one knows that they are going to go through 'the
torments'. A first year of it ended in late Autumn of
Orwell's Burmese jungle. (Orwell, drop your loin
cloth.) I cannot see in the dark.

You, whoever you are but obviously a drugged papist;
me as close as a young girl, dying. One on stage all
during this time; I had a dream you were oldstar,
oyster, tenor McCormack. I read the description on
the gate of your last house (in my next to last – at
jungle's edge) 'Fountain of the Papal Court'.

Everything is happening in a shebeen, hillside fields
speaking easy. A seminary is full of semen, but here
move harvests gallants in gorgeous dresses. The
cover of the harper's field that hides its own insects.
Too clever for the clover – me!

The torments of one October to another in a jungle
line. Defiling. It's as well one cannot see in a dark
hairy nest. Dear Barf of my country, one must
concentrate on props. Concentrate on the props of
the non-existence of months.

RICHARD
LIVERMORE

Foregoing Sundering Swords for Completeness

the nosey eye of the morning's shaft
searches rooms with a powdered glare.
love lies low
where manned bodies lurch
to herald the taut.

two lovers love
ringing bedclothes above
two warriors bulging beneath.
pantic dawn,
and down in the woolly cave
Achilles and Hector
strapple,
advancing milky ways.

angled to probe and rocket to
soft space, these astronauts are
a favoured race.
brute strength purrs
from fabled arms
of combat-courted men
come to the colosseum.

tigers muscles' rising rivids
swell to the kill. bronzed blondes
with tanklike torsoes
mell to the Fuhrer's will.

at home in command
of strappling soldiers, she dotes
on a race of muscular men's
metal-matted shoulders to swoon.

in the Congo, Major Mike Whore
was a real lady who disliked
nancy-boys, and said:
let me have real men about me.
she chose sinuous Africans, to boot,
and riddled their bodies
with envious bullets.

greased shirts, torsoes hiding,
zealously guard a factory's virility.
looking-glass boys
in a working-class guise
flex to admire.
but it is strained stuff.
the rays of these sons
are glazier filtered.

he struggles to cope – alsatian leashing.
biceps, graunching, tigers tether
and drag to a heel! or a heil!
a chain makes a gasping dog
choke back rage till a child is savaged.

they lie there still, in bedclothes moduled,
engined to purred, trajectoring down.
encapsuled together, foregoing
sundering swords for completeness,
they splash in a milky ocean,
waft and lock
while the world hunts them down.

For Cowards and Traitors

down as deep as under these sheets
where warrior-lovers
wipe off their blades
and, done with their service,
relax, I dreamt
a highly apposite
dream in a hut
cemented with shit:

U-Shaka, tall as the sky,
surveying his soldiers
who, rather than die
for cowards and traitors,
kept up the vigil
of war and the barracks
in beds where only
the dead could relax.

EDWARD
LUCIE-SMITH

Yes, I write this poem in

Yes, I write this poem in
secret, not from you, but from
myself. Look, I say, I have
escaped your black art, words mean
just what they say, and no more.
Yet my notebook calls. Some-one
is late, the mind is idle.
I scribble, chaotic strokes
scarcely creating letters.
Let us pretend this is
not happening, a poem
is not being born. The spell
is not cast or, if it is,
has nothing to do with love,
dearest love, nothing at all.

It's the season for broken hearts

It's the season for broken hearts.
The trees in the park stripped bare,
the streets sordid
with old cans, broken bottles,
yellowed newspapers reporting
those glorious days last year
before our fates collided.
We sit home and examine our hurts
to see if they are hurting,
and wait for the phone-call
which will resume our war –
dominance and submission,
the silences of battle
as each waits for the other
to announce a new position.
Then a bird chirrups 'Why bother?'
on a branch that's still naked.
A stranger comes to the door
with the necessary gift of danger.

Sleepily murmuring, not

Sleepily murmuring, not
certain as yet what manner
of pleasure this is, or if
it is part of your dream or
the waking to come, you turn,
arrange yourself, and accept
the sensation. And I,
uncertain, not of the act,
but whether I've been given
permission to enter
and mingle myself with what
you are dreaming, advance
like a child in a game, two steps
forward, one back, until I
am sure of a welcome. You
open your eyes, suddenly,
and I am caught out, stumble,
drown in the turbulent blue.

The Accusers

Young men in California
displaying themselves to the lens –
fifty thousand wet dreams
to every blink of the shutter.
They are so shining,
so proud of their beauty –
white teeth, smooth buttocks,
and there, at the point of focus
'endowments' rising up,
as if magnetised, pointing
directly, so directly,
at us, the accused.
The heads of accusation:
lack of youth, lack of beauty,
which they too will lack
almost directly.

JOHN
McRAE

Elijah and Isaac

Isaac and Elijah
Were a beautiful couple.
Lived in Jackson, Mississippi.
We met them: Went to see
Dressed to Kill

Loved it

Went home. Ate
Creole,
Made love.

Kept in touch
Three years.

This June Elijah died of AIDS.
This is not a poem about Elijah dying of AIDS.
I love the memory of him.

But God I weep for Isaac.

When Did You Last Look For Your Father?

(for Thom Gunn)

Did you ever look for your father?

I found mine one night in the pub
On his back under a table singing,
Feet up, kicking the table in time with the song,
A small hole in the back of his trousers
Halfway down the right thigh, his kicks
Spilling beer and glasses into the sawdust
Sticking to him and to the floor.

Maybe he wasn't the one after all.

I found him another time
Shovelling snow, determined
There were sheep trapped in the drifts
And working towards them in huge cold silence
In motorbike gauntlets and a heavy black coat
With a scrape of white paint on it
Different from the snow. And he
Couldn't hear me because of the wind.

But maybe that wasn't him either.

   Then the time we went fishing
   He stood in the torrent, great
   Black waders black water round them,
   And I lost my balance, so did he
   Trying to catch me. On the way
   Home he put his hand on an electric fence.

What was it I wanted to remember him as?

Leaning out of a train arriving
Tossing his bag, a large canvas bag, ex-navy, to me
And I dropped it.
He came to me, three was I, four? Bent down, his
Hat brim pushed against my head, I turned away.
I think now then I saw hurt in his eyes
Neither he nor I understood or expressed.

To forget to remember. Maybe that's him. Or was.

Fall

Does a ship need a rail
To stop the people falling off?

I have this image of lots of people
Falling off ships and balconies

If there weren't any rails.
Like old ladies off bus platforms
Going round corners

Yo-yos off strings
Planets off orbits

The whole world going off the rails.

Man made rails for direction and enclosure.

But there seems to have been this great
                              Falling off.

Poem?

Part of the trouble
Is reading other poets.

That touch of fashionable angst
Sets my teeth on edge

And the rediscovery of Nature's been done before.
Childhood in the fifties

Or Childhood in the sixties
Comes to much the same

We need a new *Howl*,
As we have always done.
The stories are the same
And the needs never change.
1798/1987/8676087.

Shall I tell you a story I asked.

I once saw a drunk man killed
On the Glasgow subway.
His coat caught in the doors
As the train moved away
And he slipped between
Train and platform edge,
Dragged, screamed, a siren went.
Howl.
Doesn't matter to him I saw him die.
                              I grew up a bit
In October 1958,
My first week
In the big city.

ZIGGY
MARSH

Fighting For Your Life

Fighting for your life
means lips sticked
and black nails, well
cut and hair long.
Still a man underneath.
Single names and genderless
women's names like goddesses
throw your public into giggles
of delight. Confusion.
Life fighting maybe seems
a night time occupation
but daytime parties do stalk
the street fishnetted and green.
Studs thrust themselves into
your back and demand to be seen.

Life fighting is a pointless
waste of time and fighters
of life are pressganged
into macho poses, knuckles
poised and jabbing!

I stay home.
Watching reality on tubes
four-sided. Allow my dreams
to be recorded
and dye my skin magenta.

Lipstick Dreamer

As a kid he played
in the closet.
Dressed in gingham
and musquash and loved it.
Lipstick lips he mouthed
and pouted at
strangers who came to tea.
He was cute and the strangers said Aahh!

At nine he wore
his mother's best frock.
Danced in the garden
ignoring the clock.
Lipstick lips he mouthed
and pouted at
strangers who came to see.
He was smacked and the strangers said Aahh!

When fourteen came
he was into stilettos,
fishnet tights and bulges
on photos hidden away in drawers.
Lipstick lips he mouthed
and pouted at
strangers who came to pee.
He was drunk and the strangers were free.

Poor Old Athol

At school poor old Athol
wounded look, minced around
nose in books. People picked
and kicked and teased him
burnt his fingers
pinched and squeezed him.
Athol never said a word
Athol always turned away.
Poor old Athol on the
sports field, sliding, slipping
in the mud. Never saved or
kicked the ball once,
never even touched the ball.
Later in the showers he shivered
scared to show his skinny bum.
Poor old Athol
poor old schoolkid
I never even spoke to him.

Poor old me, another poof,
walked around head in the roof;
had my mates, the tough
the butch ones.
No one ever dared
touch me. Me, a prefect,
doing maths homework for
all the other hostile schoolboys.
On the sportsfield I
had a headache
didn't even touch the ball.
In the showers my mate
would kiss me and touch

my balls if I touched his.
Poor old Ziggy.
Poor old Athol.
What a shame. How sad.
What have we missed?

Mr X

In the back of an antique shop
surrounded by precious pieces
I sit on a something chair
and eat chocolate digestive biscuits.

They sit on a Staffordshire plate
perched gingerly on my lap.
Mr X goes to see to the door
and says he'll soon be back.

He teaches me art at school
and takes me out to tea.
I'm just seventeen
and he is thirty-three.

I stay behind at four
and help him tidy up.
He always locks the door
I let him touch me up.

In the back of his antique shop
surrounded by precious pieces

I sit and watch the clocks
while he sells the marble Jesus.

He takes me to the Royal;
we have coffee, cakes and toast.
He likes to entertain me.
He likes to play the host.

When he took up another post
it didn't stop us meeting.
We'd still have coffee and cake
on Fridays at two sittings.

In the back of his antique shop
surrounded by precious pieces
I tell him it's got to stop
my parents have got suspicious.

In the back of an antique shop
I come with another male.
There's wet on the wonderful Wedgewood
and sperm on the Chippendale!

DAVID
MAY

Observation 1

Oh,
    how I wish you'd try to catch my eye,
And look,
       and stare,
           and talk without moving your lips:
But you don't.
And you,
Yes you in the corner on your own.
Smartly dressed,
Although there's something in the way
You keep adjusting your jacket which tells me
This man loves himself,
          more than he could another.
Next to you sits a youth,
         with a cigarette.
He's quite plain.
I like this one;
Ordinary,
    yet he would not be so inside,
Each has a tale to tell and thoughts hidden,
          and secret.
And I'd like to hear them.
Go on,
    speak to me.
Spend the night clearing your conscience
          over a drink.

And from then on I shall think of you,
Each time a misty-blue cloud of smoke stings my
    nostrils.

The lads,
    with jeans and muscle,
                    and checked shirts,
                    and vests.
All in a group
            looking over at some bright,
                        young,
                            thing.
Not tried and tested yet.
Heaven help you my friend,
                    entering this unknown,
And with it
A new sexual experience,
                not liked the first time,
                but you will,
At least you say you will,
They all do.

Where Are You Now?

The memory fades,
                slowly and surely,
It fades.
Like the half remembered musical theme
winding,
    swaying in the mind

Until all it leaves are a few notes of identity.
This is how you recede from me.
Only brief moments tether us now,
                though these will never weaken.
Each recollection fills a cave in my mind,
lines it with incidents,
                thoughts,
                        words,
                            emotions.
And when you left me this chamber closed forever.
No other can enter.
Its contents slumber,
                almost,
Though echoes of you still reverberate around the
    walls.
From outside I can hear so faintly,
                            this laughter,
                            this voice,
                            these sweet words,
Teasing and torturing me,
reminding me of this half filled emptiness,
            of something incomplete and unfinished,
Uncontrolled,
            independent,
It lies inside.
Then,
Sometimes,
Very rarely and when least expected
A charmed key opens the lock.
A sight,
    an odour,
            music,
A special aura in the air

And for so brief an instant I am in ecstasy.
The outside world recedes,
Starlight descends,
In a swirling rhapsody forgotten memories stream
    afresh, flooding my mind.
And I am one with you,
                    once again.
As I am transported to happier times
I dance,
I sing,
I caress,
I kiss.
Gentle breath.
Softly we touch,
        softly we communicate,
And so softly in my heart the ache of love returns;
This reverie is double edged,
For I feel my love and pain together.
At once enjoying you and afraid at your transience,
And,
Slowly,
    ever so slowly,
Though still too quickly,
The door closes by degrees,
                    unhurried,
Until the dream is broken.
It has withdrawn,
            unto its cavern
All I can hear,
        once again,
        are its vibrations through the walls.
The glittering light sets to dusk.

The pervasive resonance of love,
of happiness;
Livened,
light,
Dissipates to nothing.
Here I sit and revert to my daily task.
For this brief time I felt life quicken its pace
And now its sedate tumble reasserts itself.
The memory fades,
slowly and surely,
It fades.

THOMAS
MEYER

Valentine

Scarlet, crimson. 'Laurel'
or rhododendron leaves
hung like panatelas
loosening

rolled by the chill
let go a little
after this bitter
cold, a thaw

relaxes each leaf
slightly. A cardinal
darts
up from the wood, flickers
in a leafless tangle

up for the millet, wheat
cracked corn
at the feeder. What
do I ache for

that turns up
like that?
Unexpected and suddenly
red?

Occasion

As the sun moves through the trees
outside the window, the window where
we sat, often, and moves behind
the hills, it traces with red

the houses across the street. The love
(Dante agrees) that moves the sun
moves me in the quiet dark of five
after five, this grey December day.

Letter From the Western Isles, Scarista

Here in the Hebrides everything
was autumn-colored until
today, the deep blue sea with yellow sand
and tiny shells the exact

pink in the whorl of your ear.
Because of longing, those flecks
of white the wave leaves in its wash
or that lacy curtain flapping

in the bathroom window gently
and I am breathless
reminds me of you.
Not to mention the moon

the other night about two
a fierce orange and nearly full
and when I looked again
she wasn't there.

By a Sleepy Lagoon

Cantal finally! How long has it been?
I've wanted some since the Auvergne. Somewhere
else I had it . . . a restaurant, Vienne
or maybe I mistook the rind (could have been
the once dans l'Auvergne). Ah Cantal, simple
nutty, much milder than Cheddar, ivory
good in omelettes, not so harsh as Gruyère.

I drift, fat, content, limply on a raft. Faraway names.
Haven to the least of my whims (as long as they're
    foreign)
come Hell or Highwater, I can't resist shiftless
    wishes.
October tomorrow, Fall. And what will that bring?
Color? Lush yearning? A sad ordinary
sense of things coming true. Day long daydreams
not caring if I ever eat Cantal again.

CARL
MORSE

Dream of the Artfairy

One day over the course of a week or so,
all the art made by fairies
became invisible to straights,
starting with the Sistine Chapel.
It was mid-July, and thousands of riled up visitors
demanded an apocalypse or their money back,
although it was noticed certain persons
continued to point and giggle at the ceiling
– for the fairies could still see perfectly well.

Then the Last Supper went.
And some noted art historians tried to get their vision
    back
by clumsily attempting a gross indecency or two,
and traffic in forged fairy papers became a nightmare.
But nothing worked
– except for the ethically dubious practice
of tempting real fairies to simulate
the shapes of the Elgin marbles.

Then to indelible effect
a Tchaikovsky symphony disappeared
in the middle of Avery Fisher Hall,
but for a piping fairy here and there
who could still read the music on the page
and one panicky but determined violin.

And the bins of Sam Goody bulged
with the unsold silent discs of Broadway hits,
and hum-along fairies ruled the Met,
and take-a-fairy to Tanglewood clubs were formed,
in case any Brahms or Ravel was played,
and the first Easter passed without even one
   'Messiah'.

And then in the classroom of our days
the fairy voices died – in mid-pronunciation. So:

– I taste a liquor never brewed
  from tankards _____ ____ _____,
– The mass of men lead lives ____ _____
  _____,
– A rose is a rose ____ __ _____,
– They told me to take a _____
  _____ _____.
– Out of the cradle _____
  _____,
– Call me _____,
– Oh, Mama, just look at me one minute as though
  you really saw me . . . Mama! Fourteen years
  have gone by! – I'm dead! – You're a
  grandmother, Mama – . . . I married George
  Gibbs, Mama! – Wally's dead, too. – Mama! His
  appendix burst on a camping trip to Crawford
  Notch. We felt just terrible about it, don't you
  remember? – . . . But, just for a moment now
  we're all together – Mama, just for a moment let's
  all be happy – . . . Let's _____ ____ _____
  _____!*

*If you filled in any of the above, even in your head,
you may be a gifted fairy.

And the publishers failed when so many books
went blank in mid-fulfillment,
and no-one but fairies passed their bar exams.

At last only Robert Taylor kept making love
to the hole where Garbo used to be,
and a touchdown pass in the closing game
never reached its tight end on the screen,
and all hell really broke loose in the land.

And the Good Fairy saw that it was bad,
or at least not so hot,
and that a sense of justice can go a long way.
So she kicked the transmitter
and the straights woke up restored.
And the earthfairies didn't mind so much,
since they had more time to draw
– and interpreting isn't the best of jobs,
no matter how you get paid.

scooped in pearl (Emily Dickinson)
of quiet desperation (Henry David Thoreau)
is a rose (Gertrude Stein)
streetcar named Desire (Tennessee Williams)
endlessly rocking (Walt Whitman)
Ishmael (Herman Melville)
look at one another (Thornton Wilder)

West Street Story

The latest squad of kill-a-queer-for-Christers with
  Jersey plates
picked out another sissy to surround with 'Going
  somewhere, faggot?'
But another queer noticed, and another,
and an ill-tempered knot of faeries too thick to fight
  a way out of grew,
and adhesive tape appeared,
and a quiet march to the docks ensued,
and their clothes came off.
And a voice said suddenly 'let 'em go'
so we could watch their eyes
look hopeful for a while;
and then we loaned them suitable stuff
while we did to them what queers are taught
to do to each other in bathtubs and slings,
including some permanent messages.
And then we took our stuff back and undid just
  their feet
and played an experimental pansy game
with them and their own cars around the piers
until it became a terrible chore
of how to prevent them from being under the
  wheels.

Fairy Straighttalk

– to Jerry Falwell
– to Patrick Buchanan
– and to the couple who stared with deliberate contempt,
   disgust, and loathing at four gay men in my
   neighbourhood restaurant on April 8, 1983 (five days after
   Easter, three days after Passover)

– letting us know for certain you didn't want that
   kind of Jew
spreading cancer in *your* restaurant
as if they owned the place,
even asking for more bread,
almost biting off your lipstick
in your haste to
slam on your fur and exit with a ramrod back.

May the next AIDS donor
to spit down your throat
be your son and heir,
yes, the one who never forgets
your cake or smile.
May he be one of the three-piece men
who daily get faggots to gulp their loads
in bushes and gyms and picture shows,
in the front seats of out-of-town coupe de villes
and the back seats of full-service Burgerpits,
and in everyone's stockroom after five.
May you presoak the Pampers of such a tyke,
and may he get tagged by your friendly guard
who will send you duplicate restroom snaps
to paste on the page with the cap and gown
and the bride and sweethearts who must bear
your history and genes,

as well as a super-colour-eight
of junior on your bedroom wall
moaning SUCK IT, SUCK IT, SUCK IT
before zipping up quick and thanking you
as he exits the dump or parkway lot
heading home for a nourishing warm-up dish
and helping the kids with homework math.
And may every faggot he ever traded
kisses, cocks, and caresses with
show you their assholes in their dreams.

As for you, sir, training half your back
and undercurled sneer and lip on us,
may your gate be guarded by a muscle fruit,
may your flag be folded by an anthem queer,
may a service pansy lead your prayers,
may a paper faggot deliver to your door,
may a spelling fairy promote your kids,
may a navigation faggot steer your flight,
may your call be routed by a switchboard queer,
may a justice fairy adopt your case,
may a thirsting faggot fill your mug,
may your car be inspected by a wrench fairy,
may a hammer faggot build your house,
may a power pervert buzz your station,
may a federal finkfaggot target *your* population
for a nationwide screen test
– and when you have your straight, white heart
    attack,
may your eyes, rolling wildly about the ward,
find only a lifetime faggot nurse for help,
and a bedpan fairy and oxygen aide,
and a really pissed-off healthfaggot
with the nitroglycerin bottle
at an unreachable distance from the bed,
holding the cap down tight.

And may thus you recover the signal range
of how much a regular kiss can do,
how many clubmates have Herpes Two,
and what you produced in the dream of the girl
who didn't want only a football fuck,
while 'fooling around' in the pop-up tent,
not hiding a hard-on in the pool,
but beating the shit out of any guy,
or woman or child who had the cool
to look in your eye,
or ask you why.

On the basis of your table manners alone,
I think it best we not compare
breeding or education,
since only one of us seems to know
that Nazis are made not born.

PHILIP
MYALL

Eddie's Shorts

Eddie wore these shorts
And I remember him
A different kind of man from me

Eddie was not beautiful or clever, but
He had a kind heart
In his lean and handsome sportsman's frame

I think about his body
Pulling on the shorts and doing up the buttons
As before the mirror I do now

And every part of him
His long spine, ankles, pliant sleeping member
Full of a simple and undaunted being Eddie

Yet always from his goofy grinning mouth
There sprawled a desperate joking
And I would not want to be him, though I wear his
    shorts

For in that laughing sadness
Lay no inkling of quite how the world failed him
Not equipping him to live in it, but only

As a clumsy man inside a cultivated body
To lord over it
From first steps taught he should

Accomplish life, as he accomplished games
In these black shorts I stole from him
To wear them, knowing he had worn them

I still fool enough
To think of reaching after his confused man's heart
Through his uncomplicated body

Not because I loved him
But because I would have fucked him
Given half the chance

A man myself and made as badly
Safe inside the games I learned as Eddie learned and
    laughing
Even in my own shorts

Sirens

Leaves that clatter, cans
Collect beneath the railing

Boys collecting
Utter cries like code

They rattle words
Like someone else's keys, all

Speaking with limbs
The simple messages of lust or violence

A talisman of meat
The hard cock or the fist, they flex

Between strength and suffering
Their wank

Is a bouquet of rage
They come blood

Fear disports within the pleasure gardens
Their confusion calls upon the corner

Wind blows
And another siren

Look
They are at sea in the boat of longing

But where to go
What wind will carry

PAT
O'BRIEN

Get Out

There he sits
totally alone
a topic of conversation
never given a chance
to express or feel
never looked upon
except to tease and mock

I look, I see no ill
only a schoolboy
alone in thought
tormented from without
as from within.

He smiles warily
half expecting –
astonished that
it is returned
conversation begins.
Anger, despair, puzzlement
then it's out:
He's gay
They Know
Cannot prove
Work on assumption –
any excuse will do –

Life is Hell.
How can he accept
How can he begin
How does he realise
Being gay is no sin?

Step into the unknown
Out of the closet
Before the air runs out. Or
another wasted life
never known love,
a person that cared,
a fellowship of understanding.
How does he accept
How does he find
When all thoughts wretched?
And being gay the cause?
No. The cause is them –
the heterosexual machine
grinding down 'waste'.

So, shine like diamond
and love too
never forget, you are you.

Winds

Unearthly energies past me fly
Howling winds to freeze my soul
I shall not repent
Hurriedly down slippery street I travel
Towards home's haven of warmth
My soul colder, colder
Then I see silhouettes
Under a haggard tree
Two men embracing, loving
My soul melts, the winds retreat.

FELICE
PICANO

Progeny

Sometimes, not often but sometimes
I think about the boy-child I never had
The child I would have sired if my semen
Hadn't slipped down youths' throats
Smeared men's moustaches, lodged
Around bends up their asses.

By now he'd be in school, maybe ten
Or eleven, fifth grade or sixth
If he's smart as I was then. Smart ass
As I was. Always looking for trouble.

Would he have my eyes, my mouth?
Any of the thoughts I gather inside?
Would he come upon Homer, suddenly,
Looking at the Flaxman drawings for hours
As though they might explain that tale of gods
And heroes too noble, too bad to be true?

Would he wonder, staring out the window
At snow, why he arrived here, with us,
Born out of his mother and I
And not, say, in some suburb of Spain?

Would he be fat or thin? Athletic
Or bookish? Would he build miniature

Rockets, make chemical experiments?
Or prefer parties, sniffing glue in basements?

Would he glare at me, if I came into a room
Unexpectedly, as at a stranger.
Ever think to write a poem. Laugh at me
For doing so? Or would he be proud
And tell his buddies in a voice half
Awed, 'Hey, Dad's been published again!'

Not that it would make a difference really
If I had a son, what with fresh new nephews
And nieces, close enough when I want their youth
Distant enough to cause few problems.

But sometimes I wonder what it would be like
To grow up in China on a communal farm
Or in Kamchatka, chewing Sea Lion skin,
And sometimes I wonder if he'd look at me –
Slumped in a chair – and turn away, knowing
He would be better, his upper lip curled in scorn.

Birth Marks

We are astonished and pleased
by human imperfection –
The mark from within that
dewlaps into distortion – the girl with the oaktree
    hair
The man with cobra penis –
We are amazed, superior, content.

But listen, we all bear a mark
as though genes burst at birth
into signature
saying look, this is new,
individual, despite rules,
accomplished again.

My own is a splatter of rash
two inches long, left bicep.
Over decades it has stood as proof:
when young of desired Cherokee
blood, later – a swan in flight –
that the ugly duckling had fled.

Clear, bold, exposed – brown
when I'm tanned, scarlet when pale,
I kiss it for luck in showers,
touch it in private passing
obvious monsters:
reiterate my uniqueness.

Odd that friends seldom see it,
lovers discover it the morning
we say farewell, odd that my mother
– who must have washed the spot –
only recently noticed it, asked
if I'd been burnt. Yes, I told
her. Into being. Burnt into life.

Window Elegy 3

Ice cracks every atom of our leather jackets.
Giant granite ladies far too plumply unclad
primp across the unraked gravel. Our flimsy
chairs tilt and softly sway, slightly out of synch.
We are alone again, after three hours of people
– living and avoided, threaded through; or greatly
dead, their artifact souls impanelled for us
to try ourselves before. A late December afternoon
is on display.

                Windows surround us on three sides.
Four, if you count the sheer glass behind the stone
wall we sit in front of: a curtain that will never rise:
No more scenes shall follow. Kertesz might have
photographed us here. From on high, perhaps,
   picking
out five bare trees, little storms of paper
swirling, two bundled seated men, not talking.

We are though, words the wind slaps across our
   faces
honing scarves to razor edges. Our voices are low
concrete cold. We could be plotting a hold up
or government's overthrow. Over one point so often
before in our separate thoughts we're both
   embarrassed
somewhat bored. Each freshly said phrase comes
   out
pre-arranged.

              I count forty-eight windows.
People can be seen if we shade our eyes from the
   frozen

light that blanks first this then that glass expanse.
Women in knitted caps, coats dangling. Ringed
    moons
above decaying landscapes. Men checking their
    watches.
Dali's driven, ever falling crucifixion.

You are a new you: uncertain, unpleading. This
showdown hurts. A spot of red has already bruised
your right temple. I would lick it white. But
that would mean surrender. Even so, you are more
beautiful than ever, now that I have chosen to lose
    you.

When we rise from our seats, my ungloved finger
brushes your cheek. We will pull apart soon
and – like a tongue upon sub-zero steel – we will
    bleed
for years. Windows around us splatter with sun
like flashbulbs exploding as a Rock Star descends
or a madman with a machine gun, as he first opens
    fire.

NEIL
POWELL

At the Edge

Far inland this late July,
I imagine those coastlines –
Caernarvon, Sussex, Suffolk –
and think of you at the edge
of a well-studied ocean
whose dirty secrets emerge
numbered in tomato pips.

Through a vocabulary
which does what it has to do
with ungraceful exactness,
you express about the sea
things I shall never fathom,
confronting those mysteries
whose gift is their remoteness.

And yet, awed, intransigent,
I too must question; concoct
in the kitchen of ideas
the approximate flavour
of some finely-charted coast;
season it with the right words.
Scientist and writer are

not so different, perhaps. . . .
Men who live on their edges,

inhabit borders, margins,
embody the coasts they crave
and need the answering clash
of waves over the shingle,
no metaphor but design.

The Bridge

One stands above an upstream cutwater,
Rod angled aimlessly towards the land,
Safe in his niche; while on the other side
His friend leans on the opposite pilaster,
Arms braced against the stone and legs astride
As if to clasp the bridge with either hand.

There are no fish. The first knows this and smiles:
It is enough to be a part of air
And sun and stone and water, bridging them.
His line into the river runs for miles,
Transfigured from the rod's initial stem
Into the web of currents everywhere.

His friend feels none of that. He stares downstream
Where sunlight catches an abandoned tyre
And glances back in glossy insolence,
Hardened into a rigid silver gleam.
The clasp upon the parapet grows more tense.
Sweat chills his neck. The stonework is on fire.

Between the bridge's piers the river brings
Its casual luggage and its fluent art
Past those whom it will neither curse nor bless:
One is detached because a part of things,
The other restless in his separateness.
The bridge which bears them carries them apart.

Studies

1

A dimly disinfected corridor
Leads back into the past, through ember light
From old bulbs nested in red plastic shades.
Its intersections tempt with dark dead ends:
Cracked and clattering pantry, endless cellar,
Deep cupboards housing colonies of shoes.
There's no escape nor whimsical detour.
The furniture of fear. The silent door.

2

Trust's emblems: open doors, plain Seniors,
Freedom of uncharted bookshelves – this
Was all the world I wished to grow into.
Up skeletal boxed stairs to attic rooms
Where adolescent literati met
And unregarded age hung in the eaves:
Contained or cobwebbed by indifference,
We traded in our different innocence.

3

The six bells tumbled over misty elms
To summon the devout, unnoticing
A grey cat in the hedge, a dew-lit web,
And a boy behind the leaded window, writing
At this desk, studious in another house.
I see him now, and want to say, 'Don't worry,
The years will heal your broken images.'
The whirligig of time brings his revenges.

4

A midland window framed another view:
Suburban trees, back gardens, washing-lines
And afternoon sun sliced by venetian blinds.
Books, records, papers tried to lend a name
To stateless furniture: identities
Lodged tentatively in a no-man's land.
The sudden warmth of strangers: good to find
Such kindness shown to one not of their kind.

5

An attic in a tall and silent house,
The wrong end of town, defining solitude:
I lived, consoled by anonymity,
For six safe months – deliberate prelude
To garret life, I thought. Enough of that:
Long evenings in the Roebuck; coming of age;
A few friends in the hazy rooms; below
The trees in Eastnor Grove were hunched with
    snow.

6

The streetlamps flickered out in Distons Lane.
Above the arch, we played our dangerous game
Through smokey nights and aimless faded days,
Watching ourselves or the receding room,

114

Booklined, Cotswold-stoned. It seemed enough:
Talk, music, whisky, dope, a little art,
Steps echoing in the archway; high above,
He said something or other about love.

7

A hamlet called The Town. And Matthew said,
'If I lived in a place like this, I'd write.'
We crossed the river meadows from the Crown,
Returning homeward through the mellow night,
Then talked on in the open-windowed room
Where honeysuckle weighed upon the air;
Knew nothing of the imminence of loss,
An accidental end, time's double-cross.

8

Suddenly space: high ceilings and white walls.
Perhaps I thought a change would set me right –
Simple as that. False logic of facades,
An each-way bet, a love at second sight,
The liar's self-conviction of a truth:
Thus caution tempts desire to leasehold life.
Bland architectural graces, signs misread:
Within, some space stayed uninhabited.

9

Now darkness has closed in around the desk.
The night's surviving colonists stand guard –
An angled lamp and a low-glowing fire
Where random bricks are blackened by old
     smoke.
Scotch, coffee, and the final Brandenburg:
At last a little time belongs to us.
Outside, the street is sobered, still: it's late;
The house's timbers gently ruminate.

IVOR
C
TREBY

Image of Violence

at first sight
a welded white triangle
dark vortexed against a black
background, involuted
cushioned, bulge-tight

almost
a sphincter

then his
(whose) flexed
arm, pumping –
deltoid, biceps, extensors,
brachioradialis

not *musculus*
but plump rats running

(and) tattooed
a blue lit eagle
climbing the forearm
talons raked, plummetting
skyward

a species rapacious,
protected

last
the bladed fist
the fury channelled down
through brain
eye, wrist

a skewering knife
to stab, to flay

this is Garuda
american style
black hair mossing at
throat, jaw
axilla

a dagger
but no *amṛta*
observe his ear
that too is prominent
tuned to the high thin
scream (homo
interfector)

only
butchers hear

mosiac

the guy in whom my heart delights
he never calls, he never writes

he sends no word to show he cares
he lives unmoved by my affairs

i want to build, he fears I'll bind
he'll not admit me to his mind

and, choosing friends less troublesome
awaits that knight who'll never come

        i've been most gentle and correct
        perhaps he did not want respect

        less interested in heart or head
        than what we might have done in bed

        is he so blind he cannot see
        this same desire is prompt in me

        that for his sake i curb excess
        prefer to show him tenderness?

for love we both have understood
is chaste, as well as nicely lewd

sharing and mutual trust the base
on which it grows; so each embrace

other to other reconciles
harmonious as a chest of viols

i stare dry-eyed at these four walls
he never writes he never calls

118

NOLAN
WALSH

After Five Years

You lace my bed night cocoa with spiders
I mix your morning porridge with sperm

You give the press the best insiders
I've sent your photo to a porno firm

I smear my kissing lips with garlic fat
You send poison pen letters to my cat

You say talk while you walk
I say walk while you talk

You boil all my Doris Lessing novels with the
    aubergines
I've given away your best drainpipe jeans

After five years
I don't think we are friends anymore

monogamy

oh! dear, my dears, the pose-rose has
just poisoned me on monogamy
how did i slip-crack-slap
on me bum, how come monogamy?
rose-sulphur sulphur-rose burnt out
me eyes on him – nice crack of a chap

but i'm no hide-fried-tied of
a maida vale bride. oh! dear, my dears
how can i wizz-dizz-miss with the boys
(who i might add are not toys)
when i slip-crack-slap
on him – nice crack of a chap?

Twisting Out

I
In Harlem men would 'twist' the night away[1]
forbidden in the harness of the 'permissive' sixties
holding out breakfast invitations to the 'lay'
on the jockey of their strong wrists

After the 'twist' came the 'shout'
and a dance called 'The Stonewall' demanding[2]
real energy and blood
It spread to London in the early seventies;
A Hit on Earls Court streets with its easy chorus of
    'Out'[3]

II

For a time dancing was not in
as 'The Whitehouse jitterbug'
broke too many legs and was ve-ry expensive –
The dance was not practical and people got bored

After that; came a better dancing time with:
'The Hippy-Hippy Moon shake' 'SandM. Mash
    Potato'
'Queens Mince' and 'Clone drone' all Hits in their
    day

as usual –
the various stage masturbaters came and went:
Presley burst in a narcotic balloon –
Lennon became a child – McCartney became Prim –
Chubby Checker sank broken-hearted in some
anonymous corner – Strutting Jagger stayed like
healthy dirt under the finger nails of Rock Music –
And Men still danced in Harlem – New dances
demanding real body contact

Notes:

1. 'One of the several theories as to the origin of the Twist is that Harlem homosexuals, incensed at being forbidden by law to dance together in public, invented a routine of high erotic content in which there was no actual physical contact.' *Revolt into Style* by George Melly.

2. The Stonewall Bar Riots; gays fight back against police oppression in New York 1969 – Gay Liberation born.

3. The Colherne pub riots in mid-1970s Earls Court, London – gays fight back against pub and street raids by police.

ANTHONY
WEIR

To an Unknown Soldier

On a winding country road
with views across the sea
to mountains
two Land Rovers stopped in front of me

'Can I ask what you are doing here?'
(I quote exactly.
I was walking home.)
'Let me see your bag, please.'
(Poems, lubricating cream
and a bottle of La Tour Blanche
Sauternes 1970.)
'What is your name and address?'

I live here. My address, like yours,
is the vague cinema of the blind.
My name like yours is chance.

We have different, arbitrary numbers. Once
I joined the RAF. I sent a sonnet
to the Commanding Officer:
'Wings on a man don't make him a bird . . .'

Paratrooper, driving randomly with the other
paratroopers along narrow roads,
can I ask if you write poems,

drink wine, or get fucked
occasionally by mates or officers?

I walk along a switchback country road
alone: I and everyone – even
your Commanding Officer –
might be a terrorist to you

as you and almost everyone might be
terrorists to me.

Damascene

It was revealed to me in Dublin
(where the most approachable
men hang in the National Gallery)
that when you have no-one
to hug you but dreams
and earth, no-one
to hug but bullocks for slaughter,
you might as well have
Jesus as lover
and master fantastic,
teddy-bear tortured to death
by hard hugless men.

Minorities

If you sneer at Jehovah's Witnesses
Remember that they too
Were rounded up in Germany and France
And exterminated in the camps.
They wore mauve triangles.

Homosexual triangles were pink.
    'There were more of this category
    in Mauthausen than the other prisoners
    would have wished.'
                         The red-badged
Politicals were particularly annoyed
When rain washed out their triangles.

Out of the 17,700 prisoners at Mauthausen
In December 1943,
5,575 were political,
23 were Jehovah's Witnesses;
The 30 homosexual men
Were also starving battered and diseased
And 'There were more of this category
    in Mauthausen than the other prisoners
    would have wished . . .'*

*From *The Men With The Pink Triangle* by Heinz Heger.

JONATHAN
WILLIAMS

Instances of Contemporary Meilikhoposthoi
Amongst the Bleary Britons:

sorry, old chap:
Brewer's Droop . . .

●

sorry, old tup:
ewes' drop . . .

●

actually no, not tonight, thanks,
though we know Wittgenstein was gay,
I must say I'm tired out
with the thought

●

what
does that
gay lib button
mean?

it means
I might if it
meant anything

●

one dish
with exquisitely cut trousers . . .

now that postulants
have started coming to choir in pants
I think we must insist
they go to decent tailors

●

during the war
they used to say
about you Americans
'over-paid, over-sexed, and
over here'

*turn
over*

(12)

At Dowbiggin
(A Precinct of Garsdale)
There Are Places Called:
Long Jammy,
Sodom,
and Jack's Butts.

One Wonders
What Cunning Linguists
Will Make of That?

(April 15)
Seeds, Cotyledons, Clusters

(for Tom)

rooks and ash leaves
astride
black and yellow
air

                              steaming
                              cattle

                horsechestnut's
                solid shape
                against
                the Yorkshire sky

                                    bistort,
                                    blowing

the
ice flow
in
Satie's
piano

                longing performs
                all things

My Quaker-Atheist Friend,
Who Has Come to This Meeting House Since 1913,
Smokes
& Looks Out Over the Rawthey to Holme Fell

what do you do
anything for?

you do it
for what the mediaevals would call
something like
the *Glory of God*

doing it for money
that doesn't do it;

doing it for vanity,
that doesn't do it;

doing it to justify a disorderly life,
that doesn't do it;

Look at Briggflatts here . . .

It represents the best
that the people were able to do

they didn't do it for gain;
in fact, they must have
taken a loss

whether it is a stone next to a stone
or a word next to a word,

it is the *glory* –
the simple craft of it

and money and sex aren't worth
bugger-all, not
bugger-all

solid, common, *vulgar* words

the ones you can touch,
the ones that yield

and a respect for the music . . .

what else can you tell 'em?

ANTHONY
WORTH

Hiss

I play the Symphonies
I want to play

Unable to speak
What I want to say

As I listen
To the oxygen hiss

I sink down
Toward the dark abyss

To the sweet damp warmth
Of death's firm grasp

As my lungs force forth
My final rasp

I never thought
It could be like this

As I listen
To the oxygen hiss

My pulse slows and stops
As I sink away

The perfect end
To a perfect day

This is one
I could never miss

As I listen
To the oxygen hiss:

A Touch of Class

Two classless people
Discerning class from class
Not knowing classy elbow
From classy arsey arse

Two upper middles
Or are you lower middle dear?
Oh! for upper upper
But will I ever come so near?

Peasant stock! It has a ring
Or are you a suburban voidant thing?
Waste of talent waste of guts
Into routine 'Lower' ruts

Upper Lower
WE mix, so free
Two classless beings
We think are we

'Sorry Darling'
'It's OK Fine'
'Super Sweetie'
'Quite divine'

Classy quips
They flow so free
From two classless people
Such as we.

IAN
YOUNG

Adam and the Serpent

We lay in a garden,
and my dear friend, who was my lover, said,
speaking of the man he now loves –
    'Jack called me a scavenger the other day,
    when I asked him for an altar stone' –
and then was quiet for a moment, and looked alone.

I stroked our cat's nose and sniffed and
said we're all scavengers
come here to wander and gather
things to us. Then we're gone.
And my dear friend, who was my lover, looked
at me, and smiled, and ran inside to make our
    dinner.

And I stood in the grass in the cool evening
and watered the garden

until he joined me.

The Alteration

How
they are transformed,
sometimes

the faces of those
whose desire
falls through ours.

How
in those minutes they fulfil
their beauty,

an altering of the flesh,
real as birth,
a coming
into an absolution.

Their faces
as they lie below you, or
above,
gaze
into your face,
flushed with need,

desire
filling a perfection
from what was,
the partial beauty
suddenly complete,

the open countenance, the
eyes

eager with desire,
wide. Then

their look
fills with change –
a glass bowl
filling with clear water.

It is their quest
and the attainment
which transfigure.

The things
impinging on the mind,
on the features,
fall away.

What fixes
the muscles of the face
dissolves
into heated air and leaves
the unclouded visage
fresh with lust.

Infused
with what they seek,
drinking of us, they seem
their clear selves,
desire
filling a resolution
out of nearness.

What is remembered then?
A kind of innocence.

Human spirits,
sometimes,

human forms,

immediate,

absolute.

Not fallen.

Home on the Range

> 'Oh! Cisco!' – Leo Carillo
> 'Oh! Pancho!' – Duncan Renaldo

Have you ever thought about how
those handsome young heroes in the western movies
so often have sidekicks to help them,
inseparable older companions, familiar yet
oddly deferential,
always taking the lead from the younger guy?
A curious relationship when you think of it.
What keeps the older man riding just a little behind
his lean young friend?
And why does our hero keep him around?
Sometimes the sidekick is stout and cantankerous
(in which case he would be played by Edgar
    Buchanan)
and sometimes long in the tooth and funny (Gabby
    Hayes).

Or he might be wise, stoical and a little sad (Ben
    Johnson).
Best of all, when the young traveller has no name
and looks like Clint Eastwood,
his older friend is quiet, tough and hot
and is Lee Van Cleef.
Once or twice Lee has saved Clint's life in a tight spot.
Even so, Lee figures he still owes Clint.
Owes him a lot.
So gunman and sidekick ride together and
face down the opposition (they're always outnum-
    bered):
the sheriff and his posse, the bad guys, or the town.
Then they ride out when the job's done and
make camp for the night
cooking beans and bacon over an open fire,
crickets and the occasional wolf supplying the music.
They don't say much to each other, just a word or
two now and then, spitting into the fire.

So why do they ride together then, these two?
What strange hold does the young gunman have over
    his friend?
Does it ever occur to you
we never see these guys at home. Do they have a
    home?
Actually they do:
a comfortable ranch-house
with some ground around it for cattle,
dogs and now and then a young trail-hand or two
brought in to help with the chores and provide some
company.
So let's look in on them.
We'll say it's Clint and Lee this time,
just to be sexy about it.

Lee's a dangerous man but Clint
knows how to handle him and
has Lee haul in more wood while
Clint lounges in the big chair in front of the log fire,
one leg slung over the chair arm. He's
cleaning his gun and
watching his friend sweat.
He's half asleep but keen as a coyote,
a little smile playing on his lips.
He snaps his fingers and Lee
drops to his knees and
nuzzles Clint's swelling blue-jeaned crotch.
Clint takes his time rolling a cigarette.
Lee lights it, striking the match with one hand
Clint offers him the first puff. The rest is Clint's as
Lee, on his knees, has other things to do with his
    face.
Clint's strong hand ruffles the balding head between
    his legs and
a brass fly button
pops out of its slit.
He takes off his belt, runs it
through his hands like a fresh-shot rattler and
cracks it, suddenly, like a lariat.
Lee hisses and feels Clint's boot on his neck. It
    creaks.
The fire is hot on his back and rear. The saddle
lying on the buffalo rug
shines in the orange flame-light.
It'll be a long, cold night outside,
but warm in here, for them.
'I want it, boss,' Lee whispers.
The tobacco-stained hand, one finger-joint missing,
gently strokes the young gunman's thigh.
'Earn it then.'

(His eyes narrow to slits; his teeth clench.)
'Earn your pay.' (The pay packet
seems to be growing as Lee fondles it,
thinking about a bonus.)

In the bunkhouse, the new hired hands,
real goodlooking, both of them, but just boys,
have stripped to their longjohns and are fooling
    around
tying each other up with rawhide by the light of an
    oil lamp,
thinking about Clint and Lee.

Notes on The Contributors

STEPHEN BOURNE is a former teacher, turned journalist, who writes on the cinema. In 1983 he organised a season for the National Film Theatre, entitled 'Black Actors in British Cinema', and in 1985 he worked as film consultant to the GLC's Paul Robeson exhibition. His poems have appeared in, amongst others, *Staunch* magazine and *Dance to a Different Drum – Brixton Festival Poetry 1983*.

ALAN BRAYNE, born 1953, raised in the Black Country; mother a factory cleaner, father a factory worker. Currently lives in Basildon, Essex researching a Ph.D. thesis on the history of gay theatre. Plans to write a book based on this research. Regularly contributes to his local alternative magazine *Attitude*. His poems have appeared in *Smoke* and *Glad Rag*, stories and articles in *Zipper* and *Gay Times*.

PETE CHARLES, born (prematurely) July 1948 in Southend-on-Sea weighing 1lb 15 ozs now weighs 16 stone (his therapist is helping with this). At a very early age found his own culture incomprehensible and now speaks fluent Spanish instead. A closet railway enthusiast – 'It was far easier to come out as gay' – , he lives happily with three gay men in London. He has also fished at the mouth of the Orinoco river, bred goats in the west of Ireland and been an occasional Gay Sweatshop stage manager. He writes poetry purely for pleasure.

LAURENCE COLLINSON, born in Yorkshire sixty years ago, educated in Australia. Began writing poetry, plays and stories during his adolescence and has continued ever since. Has published several poetry collections and had many plays produced on radio, TV and the stage. A member of the original Gay Sweatshop collective, he contributed the name 'Homosexual Acts' to the first season and the successful play *Thinking Straight*. Currently earns his living as a psychotherapist, his pioneering gay group in this field continues.

STEVE CRANFIELD grew up in London's East End. For the past few years he has lived in inner London doing crisis intervention work with drug addicts. His works include: *A Stanzaic Life of Christopheles C.; The Barefoot Patient's Manual*; an aleatory poem, *Sentences of Augustine*; and *Music for the Soviet Minister of Culture*. He is currently working on a long poem dedicated to the composer Ligeti, entitled *Post-War Polyphony*.

THOM GUNN. 'Anglo American poet, born Gravesend 1929, first book of poems *Fighting Terms* (1954), moved to North California the same year, most recent book *The Passages of Joy*, which came out to largely derogatory reviews.'

LEE HARWOOD, born 1939, since 1967 has lived in Brighton, Sussex. In between writing and travelling has worked as a librarian, bookseller, forester and post-office clerk. Since 1963 has edited various 'little magazines' and given poetry readings in many countries. He has had twenty books of poetry published, several volumes of translations, and appeared in a number of anthologies.

JOHN HORDER has been a committed follower of Meher Baba, the Indian authority on the importance of hugging, since he and Craig San Roque attended a meeting in Pete Townshend's flat in August 1968. He completed the first Life Training in England in September 1984 and has been on the Staff twice this year. These three deeply moving experiences have completely changed his life, and for the first time ever he is running his perfectionist drama rather than have it run him all the time. He enjoys hugging David Ellis whenever he can.

MARTIN HUMPHRIES. 'Began writing poetry when a teenager but as most of it was explicitly gay remained a closet poet until the 1979 Gay Times Festival. Since then two books: *Mirrors* (1980) and *Searching for a Destination* (1982) have appeared. Whilst working at Oval House Arts and Community Centre was also a member of the Achilles Heel Collective which led directly to the publication of *The Sexuality of Men*, co-edited with Andy Metcalf. Currently I'm working on *Heterosexuality*, co-edited with Gillian Hanscombe; with Gay Sweatshop; and with my lover Ronald who runs a Cinema Archive.'

MARK HYATT 1940–1972. Claimed gypsy origin, never stayed anywhere long until a few years before his death when he lived with a friend in Blackburn. With little to no education it was in 1960 that he found delight in a typewriter and dictionary, and became obsessed with words. A new world opened in which he discovered Rimbaud with whom he felt a strong affinity. Michael Horovitz in *New Departures* (1975) wrote of him: 'He probably went as far out and brought just as much back as any other poet I've known.'

ISAAC JACKSON was born in New York City in 1955 and currently lives there. He is editor of *Blackheart*, a journal of writing and graphics by black gay men, and of a forthcoming collection of writings by gay men of colour. His writing has appeared in *Blackheart, Gay Community News, The Independent* and *The James White Review*. In greater New York he has done several readings, writing workshops, radio programmes and videos centred on the empowerment possible when the excluded demand to be included.

JAMES FALCONER KIRKUP. Ever since a boy terrified of the British, has lived abroad most of his life in most of the countries of Europe, in North Africa, the USA and the Far East, where he has been living off and on since 1959. At present Professor of Comparative Literature at Kyoto University of Foreign Studies. Poet, translator, dramatist, librettist and novelist (*The Love of Others*). Latest works are *Ecce Homo: My Pasolini*, *No More Hiroshimas*, *The Guitar Player of Zuiganji* (all from Kyoto Editions) and *The Sense of the Visit* (Sceptre Press).

JOHN LEHMANN has, in the course of a long literary career, written poems, biographies and three volumes of autobiography. He was the editor of *Penguin New Writing*, which lasted for forty numbers between 1940 and 1950, and the founder and editor of the *London Magazine* in the fifties.

JAMES LIDDY, born on the night of the long knives, was educated by monks of St Benedict and Celtic humanists of University College, Dublin. His poems have been published in Ireland by Dolmen Press and Malton Press; in the USA by White Rabbit Press, Capra Press, Hit & Run Press, Blue Canary Press and At-Swim Press. A short novel *Young Men Go Out Walking* was published in Autumn 1985 by Wolfhound Press, Dublin. His hobby is drinking with different Cinderellas after midnight.

RICHARD LIVERMORE, born 1944, attended various orphan homes and boarding schools until 1959, joined the army for six months at 15, then drifted from job to job for fifteen years. Has had one book of poems published plus numerous poems in magazines in England, Scotland and the USA. A founder member of the Scottish Writers' Co-operative which hopes to publish a book of his shorter poems in 1986.

EDWARD LUCIE-SMITH, born 1933, Kingston, Jamaica. Has lived in England since 1946. Four books of poems published with Oxford University Press, plus a number of limited editions with small presses. Editor of the Penguin anthology *British Poetry Since 1945*, first published in 1970. A heavily revised new edition has just been issued. Is otherwise well-known for his books on art, among them *Art Now*, *Art in the 70s*, *Movements in Art Since 1945* and *Eroticism in Western Art*.

JOHN McRAE, born Perth, Scotland, 1949, Cancer; universities of Glasgow and Nottingham; has lived and worked in Italy since 1974; written several books and numerous academic, or seemingly academic, articles on English literature and drama; been with partner, Jeremy Hunter since 1970; likes wine, sex and ravioli.

ZIGGY MARSH. 'My work is usually always my life – past, present & imaginary future. I can produce half a dozen poems in one go – then I may not write for weeks! Recently I have been writing about my childhood and teenage years. 99 per cent of my work is gay. Gay writers need to be able to say two men are making love & not have to make one of the men "doubtful" or "ambiguous", this is the "old school" & in my eyes most unhealthy.'

DAVID MAY. 'I am 26 years old and live in Stoke-on-Trent with my two cats: Shozan, a Havana, and Chai, a Korat. I work on a post-office counter. This is the first poetry I've had published. I tend to write only when inspired or depressed. I write from my own personal experience and all my poetry is in response to personal events or people I have met. Transient as either may be!'

THOMAS MEYER, born Seattle, Washington, 1947. Since 1968 has lived with Jonathan Williams in the Yorkshire Dales and Blue Ridge mountains of north Carolina. Translations of his have been included in *The Greek Anthology* (Penguin) and *The Penguin Book of Homosexual Verse*. *Sappho's Raft* (The Jargon Society) is his most recent book and he has just completed a set of sonnet sequences, the result of a collaboration with the painter Sandra Fisher. He knows a lot about cooking, computers and the impossibilities of qualitative metres in a language like English.

CARL MORSE, born and grew up (half French) in mill town in Maine, taught typing at Yale and poetry in Nice, translated Maurois essays and Verlaine biography, wrote lyrics/speeches for Medicine Show theatre, was director of publications, The Museum of Modern Art. Chapbooks *Dive* and *Turtleflow* from Burning Deck, Providence. Organiser Open Lines, N Y – readings by lesbians, gay men, pro-feminists. Cartoonist/author of *Pharos & Friends: A Field Guide to Fairies*.

PHILIP MYALL was born in the Lake District, grew up in South-West Wales, and lives now in South-West London. He has been widely unemployed in the worlds of theatre and film. When not being a poet he occupies himself with the writing of film scripts and the eating of marzipan.

PAT O'BRIEN. Born 1965 in South Yorkshire where he lived until 1983 when he moved to London to study for a degree in applied biology. Other interests are the fine arts, especially classical music. When not watching professional performances he tries to partici-pate in such activities with local groups.

FELICE PICANO is the author of six novels; a collection of poetry, *The Deformity Lover*; a collection of short stories and a novella. Founder and publisher of the Seahorse Press, and co-founder and editor of the Gay Presses of New York. His poetry, stories and reviews have appeared in scores of magazines and newspapers throughout the USA. The first volume of his memoirs, *Ambidex-trous*, was published in September 1985.

NEIL POWELL, born 1948, grew up in Surrey and Kent, educated at Sevenoaks School and Warwick University. Since 1971 has earned his living teaching. In addition to poems, articles and reviews in numerous magazines, his publications include two collections of poetry, *At the Edge* (1977) and *A Season of Calm Weather* (1982); and a critical book *Carpenters of Light* (1979). He has recently completed a book about the 1960s and is currently working on a study of the poetry of Thom Gunn.

IVOR C TREBY was born in Devonport, Plymouth and now lives in London. He has over 150 poems in print in both gay and mainstream publications; most recently his work has appeared in *Argo, Kunapipi, Labrys, No Apologies, Poesis, Southwest Review, 2plus2* and *The James White Review*. The song cycle *Women with Camellias* (music by Robin Bone) was performed in the 1985 Piccadilly Festival, and his poems *Miz' Pretty* was chosen in 1983 as pilot of a set issued by the Schools' Poetry Association. His first collection *Warm Bodies* still seeks a publisher.

ANTHONY WEIR, born 1941, lives and paints in remote isolation in County Down. His publications are: *Tide and Undertow* (poems), *Early Ireland – A Field Guide, Cinema of the Blind* (poems) and the forthcoming *Sex and Sin in Romanesque Sculpture*.

JONATHAN WILLIAMS. 'I could be defined as a poet, publisher of The Jargon Society, essayist, photographer, occasional walker of long distances, and aging scold . . . Since 1968 I have shared a seclusive life with the poet Tom Meyer, divided between the countryside of the Pennine Dales and the Southern Blue Ridge. Things we like about living in Dentdale? Walking the Howgill Fells and the Three Peaks Country, Theakston's bitter, Blue Wensleydale cheese, the fantastic sexual allure of gay-forsaken Cumbria, and the company of a few hill farmers and other classless, jolly eccentrics.'

ANTHONY WORTH, born 1957, lives and works in London. He first began writing poetry in 1981 and is presently compiling his first solo collection of poetry entitled 'Letters from Friends'. He lists amongst the things he likes to do – graphic and theatre design, and spending money.

IAN YOUNG, born in London, England. Currently lives in Toronto, Canada with his lover, Wulf. Publications include poetry – *Year of the Quiet Sun, Some Green Moths, Common-or-Garden Gods;* anthologies – *The Male Muse, On the Line* and *The Son of the Male Muse;* other publications include *The Male Homosexual in Literature: a bibliography, Overlooked and Underrated: Essays on Some 20th Century Writers* and most recently *Gay Resistance: Homosexuals in the Anti-Nazi Underground*.